Oriental Orthodoxy Unveiled

Oriental Orthodoxy Unveiled

Andrew Youssef, MTS, H. BA

AGORA
UNIVERSITY
PRESS

Oriental Orthodoxy Unveiled

Copyright © 2022 by Agora University Press

All rights reserved. Printed in the United States of America. No part of this book may be used or reproduced in any manner whatsoever without written permission except in the case of brief quotations embodied in critical articles or reviews.

For more information, contact: aupress@agora.ac

Agora University Press: press.agora.ac

ISBN 978-1-950831-38-8 (print)
    978-1-950831-39-5 (ebook)

Printed in the United States of America

HIS HOLINESS POPE TAWADROS II
118th Pope and Patriarch of the great city of Alexandria and the See of St. Mark.

HIS HOLINESS PATRIARCH IGNATIUS APHREM II
Patriarch of Antioch and All the East.

In memory of His Grace Bishop Epiphanius
of the Monastery of Saint Macarius, Scetis

Table of Contents

Acknowledgements vi

Forward viii

Preface 10

Chapter 1: Why does Theology Matter? 13

Chapter 2: Jesus Christ 18

Chapter 3: Tradition of the Church 34

Chapter 4: The Holy Trinity 49

Chapter 5: The Church of Christ 56

Chapter 6: The Sacramental Life of the Church ... 79

Chapter 7: Christian Anthropology 107

Chapter 8: Orthodox Worship and Prayer 170

Chapter 9: Sainthood: Martyrdom, Marriage, and Monasticism 182

Epilogue 190

Appendices 192

Bibliography and Further Readings 252

About the Author 260

Acknowledgements

This book you are about to read is the result of years of studying and the support of numerous individuals of which I will name a few here. I would like to first and foremost thank my parents, Nagy and Ereini Youssef. Thank you for encouraging me to pursue the field I truly love, Theological Studies. I would not be where I am today if it were not for your love and support.

I am indebted to His Grace Bishop Boulos who agreed to write the introduction for this book. Special thanks to Fr. Mina Youssef, priest of the Church of St. Mark and St. Demiana, whose parish and guidance have been indispensable for the development of my identity as an Oriental Orthodox Christian. My confessor and spiritual father, Fr. Kyrillos Mourad: thank you for guiding me on the path of Orthodox spirituality amidst my preoccupation with the academic aspects of theology.

I would like to thank Fr. Geoffrey Ready, who has been a father and a mentor to me in many ways as his student in the Orthodox School of Theology, for reviewing this book. Fr. Paul Guirgis and Kirollos Guirguis: thank you for taking the time to read this book, provide me with feedback, and for your endorsement. I would like to thank Alfred Fahmy, Dr. Bishoy Elgallab, and Dr. Peter Abdelmalak who helped me with the process of editing the book.

Most of all, I want to thank Contessa Giontsis, my fiancée, who was more supportive than I could have imagined. This book would not be here if it were not for your constant encouragement, your faith in me, and your beautiful talent that created the cover for this book.

Forward

"And this I pray, that your love may abound still more and more in knowledge and all discernment, that you may approve the things that are excellent, that you may be sincere and without offense till the day of Christ, being filled with the fruits of righteousness which are by Jesus Christ, to the glory and praise of God."

Philippians 1: 9-11

There are those who think that for a subject to be addressed properly, many ornamenting words and embellished sentences need be used. The true expert, however, will have come to know—usually after gaining much experience—that it is often the simplest expressions, communicated plainly without superfluous fuss, that offer the most clarity with regards to what is meant, and what has always been meant.

Our son Andrew N.A. Youssef has set to introduce the reader to Orthodoxy as it has been expressed and maintained by the family of Oriental Orthodox churches, ever since Christ our God-The God-Man-emptied Himself in order to give Himself up for the life of the world. We believe that he has done so most adequately, with clarity and simplicity, bringing together into a cohesive whole all the inseparable aspects of true theology: dogma, history, ecclesiology, mystagogy, culture, et al.

It brings much joy to our hearts to see such work come to fruition, and hope that it may be a blessing to all those who read it with an open heart, that love may abound still more and more in knowledge and all discernment, as the apostle says, approving the things that are excellent.

Bishop Boulos

Bishop of the Coptic Orthodox Diocese of Ottawa, Montreal, and Eastern Canada

Feast of the Lord's Entrance into Egypt
24 Pashans, 1737 AM / June 1, 2021 A

Preface

Between 2013 and 2017, I outreached university students on campus with small groups of youth attempting to introduce them to the Orthodox faith. After a few conversations, the need for a book introducing the Oriental Orthodox faith became obvious. The books available in English were mostly an introduction to a single communion within Oriental Orthodoxy rather than the Church as a whole. Between 2018 and 2019, I was blessed to give seven lectures on the Orthodox faith in a Coptic parish. These lectures covered Trinitarian theology, Christology, Anthropology, and Patrology, etc. These lectures form the nucleus of this book you are about to read.

Oriental Orthodoxy Unveiled offers an introduction to the Orthodox faith rather than a comparison between the Orthodox faith and the confessions of other denominations. As such, you will not find me comparing the doctrine of the Trinity for example as confessed by the Orthodox to the manner it is articulated in Roman Catholicism or any sect of Protestantism.

Such task is beyond the scope of this book. Furthermore, this book avoids delving into political and jurisdictional issues between the various Orthodox Churches. Only in the appendix are such issues alluded to as they pertain to each Church. This book does not aspire to resolve such issues neither does it aim to examine them as these issues have no part in the Orthodox confession of faith.

Moreover, this book does not delve into the position of the Church on contemporary issues such as abortion, euthanasia, sexual fluidity, etc. These issues, albeit important, do not constitute the apostolic faith neither are they elaborated on by Oriental Orthodox Church fathers-except in the context of church canons. Therefore, I chose to avoid these topics for the purpose of this book. If you wish to be educated on them, you can consult the synodal decrees of any of the Oriental Orthodox communions.

I hope *Oriental Orthodoxy Unveiled* be an adequate introduction for those outside the Church and are curious to join it. I hope it is an adequate resource to educate the members of each Church within Oriental Orthodoxy about the other. The Armenian, Coptic, Eritrean, Ethiopian, Malankara and Syriac communities ought to encounter one another and learn from one another. If we share the same Lord, same faith, same baptism, and same Eucharist, then there is nothing that should stop us from being educated by the fathers of one another. Therefore, this book attempted to rely on as many fathers from these Churches as much as possible to open the eyes of members of any given community to see those with whom they share the body of Christ. Geographical distance and historical events have often prevented members of the individual Churches from interacting among themselves. The age of globalization and communication ought to break these boundaries we have often suffered from as a communion. Thus, this book is a reminder to every community that the Church is greater than their ethnic community. Moreover, this book can serve youth and adult study groups within English speaking Oriental Orthodox communions hoping to deepen their understanding of the Orthodox faith. This becomes especially feasible given the easy language and low use of difficult theological terms throughout the book. Finally, I hope this book raises ecumenical awareness of the faith, history, and presence of the Oriental Orthodox Church.

Chapter 1

Why does Theology Matter?

Theology is not simply speech about God. It is a conversation or a dialogue between the divine God and the human being. No form of doing theology surpasses prayers. However, prayer ought to be performed in a manner that reflects our care about the One we speak to. God is revealed to us in the person of Jesus Christ, the Word of God. The Trinity was revealed to us through Christ in Theophany, i.e., the Baptism of Jesus. The Church found this event crucial to understanding the revelation of the Trinity. When you long for a relationship with the Trinity unto life everlasting, you begin wondering, "What is eternal life?" Jesus answers, "This is eternal life that they may know you [i.e. the Father] and Jesus Christ whom you sent" (John 17:3). Eternal life is not merely being in heaven with angels surrounding us. Ultimately, eternal life is true knowledge of God cultivated through the living experience and tradition of the Church through the Spirit in the Son. Eternal life must begin here and now to continue thereafter beyond our earthly death. Luckily, the saints who preceded us in knowledge of God left for us accounts of their experience in discourses, homilies, hymns, and liturgical texts. One way of living eternal life on earth is to take the crumps of time wasted throughout the day and convert them into times of prayers, scripture reading, reading patristic texts, and contemplation of God. Thus, the question now is where do I begin? Well, the apostles and their disciples had to answer the same question when they met those who desired to convert. They began with *kerygma* (preaching Christian life). Then, they switched to teach the *ekonomia* (economy of Christ's salvific work for us). Finally, they turned to *theologia* (dogmatic and mystical understanding of who God is as revealed in Christ). Now reading or hearing anything about these three elements of the Christian faith will be of no value if one does not struggle to live an ascetic life in which the person crucifies the flesh with its lusts and live in the newness of life offered to us through the sacraments ever flowing from the wounded side of the crucified Christ.

In other words, we must live in sacramental asceticism where the sacramental life of the church is united to our daily struggles with ourselves. We ought to live sacramentally amidst a post-modern world that perceives sacramentality as a form of superstition. In eating, you must remember the Provider of food and the One who became food for the nourishment of your soul and bodies granting Himself in the Eucharist as the medicine of immortality. In drinking, you must remember the living water which ought to be flowing from your heart. In washing and bathing, remember the cleansing of your soul through repentant tears and prayers. As you live a Christian life, read theological texts and hear sermons that will help you identify landmarks of your journey with God. Now let us return to the meaning of *kerygma, ekonomia,* and *theologia*.

Kerygma

This word refers to the preaching of the things Jesus did and said during His earthly ministry. These help you live a Christian life according to the gospel of Jesus Christ. Texts such as the Sermon on the mount in Matthew, the sermon on the plane in Luke, the commandments of Paul, Peter, John, and Jude are great biblical examples of what *kerygma* is about. Additionally, the sayings of the desert fathers are great texts of ascetical wisdom from the desert. In reading these texts, you will realize how supra-natural the Christian commandments are. Thus, you will need good reasons to apply commandments such as "love your enemies" (Matt. 5:44), "do not judge" (Matt. 7:1), "pray unceasingly" (1 Thess. 5:17), "do not look at a woman lustfully" (Matt. 5:28), etc. You will also need divine providence to apply such sublime commandments through being in Christ who, being God, lived an earthly human life.

Ekonomia

The etymology of the Greek word *ekonomia* is a combination of two Greek words *eiko* meaning house and *nomos* meaning law. This is the law of the house. When God created the world in Genesis, He was creating a house or a temple in which He would rest (as He did on the seventh day). He even placed His image amid the temple (that is the human being) just as any temple would. When this temple or house got distorted by the entrance and dominion of sin and death, the ruler of the house had to provide a "nomos" or law that can keep things in control. To the Jews, God gave the law engraved in stone through Moses. To the Gentiles, God provided a natural law written on their heart (i.e., consciousness). But at the end of the day, a law of love had to emerge through the manifestation of God to the world in the person of Jesus Christ. The birth, ministry, death, entombment, resurrection, and ascension of Christ are collectively known as *eikonomia* or Incarnation. A good example of the intersection of *kerygma* and *ekonomia* is the sermon of St. Peter after the day of Pentecost (Acts 2:14-36).

As the Word truly became man, He lived a perfect life showing humans how to attain perfection. In following Him and becoming like Him, you find the ultimate excuse or rather motivation to live the life He lived and preached. When you see Him as man living a perfect human life, you realize that you too can attain perfection not because of your works lest anyone should boast but because of His grace. You do not become sinless by nature because you sinned, sin, and will likely sin again. But you become perfect inasmuch as that is humanly possible through grace. Living this repentant life compels you to desire more knowledge of God. This is the stage at which man desire to explore *theologia*.

Theologia

When the heart has been captivated by thoughts of the divine, one seeks His face as David the Psalmist says, "When you said, 'Seek my face,' My heart said to You, 'Your face, Lord, I will seek'" (Psalm 27:8). The soul begins to thirst for

Him. One desires to cling to Him in every way possible. As such, you begin contemplating mysteries of the Trinity, the Incarnation, and salvation. At this stage, one stands before God in silence and awe. This silence should be combined with reading texts such as the theological orations of Gregory the Theologian and realize the depth of the mysteries of God. One would read *The Great Catechism* of Gregory of Nyssa and he is overwhelmed with the greatness of the Christian faith. You read the *Commentary on John* by Cyril of Alexandria and you are immersed in the theology extracted from the lengthy discourses of and about Christ. You read the mystical poems of Ephraim the Syrian, Isaac the Syrian, Jacob of Serug, and Gregory of Narek and your heart leaps with joy as your silent tongue sings the great things God has done for you.

Chapter 2

Jesus Christ

In what preceded, I have explored the sequence by which one ought to come to know God starting with the teachings of Christ through the life of Christ and ending in contemplation of the Holy Trinity. As such, I will not begin here with the classic scholastic manuals of theology where the first chapter would be about the oneness of God and the Trinity. Rather I will begin with the One through Whom we come to know God as Triune, namely Jesus of Nazareth, the Word Incarnate.

Christology

> *"[T]he immeasurable and unbearable Light... has appeared on earth today by the will of the Father, having dwelt humbly in your virgin womb, being born indescribably perfect God and Man, without being separated from the Trinity, his throne ever full of perfect glory. The One whose Divine mystery is not fully known to the heavenly hosts was made known with indescribable might to human beings."*
>
> *- Gregory Narek, A Litany for the Holy Nativity and Baptism to the Theotokos*[1]

---

[1] Abraham Terian, *The Festal Works of St. Gregory of Narek: Annotated Translation of the Odes, Litanies, and Encomia*, (Pueblo Publishing Company, 2016), 12.

The word Christology refers to what we say, live, and know about Jesus Christ according to the scriptures (i.e., the Old Testament), the apostolic witness (i.e., the New Testament), and the living memory of the Church (i.e., the Divine Liturgies, the writings of the fathers, and the councils of the Church).

Around 4 BCE, a child named Jesus was born in Bethlehem to a virgin named Mary. He was under the protection of an elderly man named Joseph and lived in Nazareth where He worked as a carpenter. Like an ordinary child, He even got lost. Unlike any other child among his uneducated counterparts, He was arguing with the elders of the temple at the age of twelve. By the time He was thirty, Jesus came to be baptized at the hands of John the forerunner. With hesitation, John baptizes Him, sees the Spirit come upon Him in the form of a dove, and hears the voice of the Father saying, "This is my beloved Son in Whom I am well pleased" (Matt. 3:17). On this day, it was obvious to John that Jesus is no ordinary man but is rather "the Lamb who carries the sin of the world" (John 1:29), who has come for the redemption of humanity. The drama of this event was so intense that some early Christian thinkers thought that this was a moment in which Jesus of Nazareth was assumed by God. However, the faith we received insists on Him being always God and that this event was but a mere manifestation of His eternal reality. After His baptism, He retreats to the desert for forty days (like Moses and Elijah). Then, He heads to Galilee and Jerusalem where He preaches the kingdom saying, "Repent for the kingdom of heaven is at hand" (Matt. 4:17). The Kingdom of God was manifested through the teachings, miracles, and encounters of Jesus. His teachings of love and forgiveness made it plain that His kingdom is not of this world. His miracles manifested that God has the upper hand and that the final word over sickness and death is His. His encounters showed that He is an ever-merciful God who is not ashamed of us despite our weaknesses. Due to His confrontations with the Jews of His time who expected a more royal and/or priestly Messiah, they plotted to kill Jesus. Having been unjustly convicted, He was framed as an enemy of Caesar and was condemned to death on a cross, a penalty often suffered by leaders of peaceful rebellion. Violent rebellions would be punishable by the crucifixion of the leader with his circle of followers which did not happen in the case of Christ. On the Cross, He is witnessed to as Son of God by a pagan centurion and as Lord by a thief. After three days, He rises from the dead and the first witnesses to such resurrection were first century Jewish women whose testimony would not be taken in a law court. The disciples hiding in the upper room would eventually arrive to the tomb to confirm the testimony of the women. In the midst of a gruesome death and disciples hiding from persecution, the Lord emerges victorious inspiring the disciples to proclaim His death and resurrection saying, "Christ is Risen, and we are witnesses of these things."

The events of the life of Jesus are primarily known through the four accounts of the Gospel: Matthew, Mark, Luke, and John. The first three overlap in many instances that they are called synoptic, meaning seen together. Matthew sheds light on the man Jesus Christ, the Jewish Messiah, in Whom the prophecies are fulfilled. Mark is giving a short account of the life of Christ as the powerful lion who sprang forth from the tribe of Judah. He emphasizes the power and dominion of Christ. Luke presents us Christ, the sacrificial calf, whose main concern is the marginalized women, tax collectors, and children for whom He offers Himself as a sacrifice. The fourth account of John gives a rather theological dimension to who Christ is as both God and man simultaneously given up by His own will for the life of the world. In all four accounts, we encounter the Word made flesh. We encounter God in Christ as much as we encounter our potential self in Him as He became a human being like us in all things save for sin alone.

The identity of Jesus Christ has been a matter of debate since the time He was on earth. He asked His disciples, "Who do people say I am" (Mark 8:27)? The answers of the disciples make it obvious that there were disagreements about who He is. This has not changed today. Some see Him as the Incarnate Word coming for our salvation while others see Him as a mere revolutionary leader and rabbi of first century Judaism. There are numerous views between these sides of the spectrum. These views aren't new. They have always been there. As such, the apostles and their disciples had to mettle with the following questions: Who do we say He is? Who is He? Is He God? Is He man? If He is both God and man, how can we describe this mystery? And the list goes on.

To settle these questions, the fathers of the Church prayed, relied on the apostles or the fathers before them, and the living memory of the Church. As wrong and selective teachings began to emerge, the Church felt the need to respond to misconceptions about who Jesus Christ is as witnessed to through the scriptures and the apostles. The responders to such erroneous teachings came to be known as apologetic fathers. The first of those would be John the Evangelist who wrote in the opening of his first letter,

> "That which was from the beginning, which we have heard, which we have seen with our eyes, which we have looked upon, and our hands have handled, concerning the Word of life."
>
> 1 John 1:1

He wrote this in response to Gnostics of the first and second centuries who taught that the Logos of God appeared in the form of flesh, yet He was without real flesh. His flesh was simply an act or a show rather than a concrete human existence. To John and early Christians, the Gnostics were compromising the reality of the Incarnation upon which the whole of Christianity is founded. As such, Gnostics came down in the lists of heretics and were not seen as Christians by the followers of Christ. Carrying the torch of combating Gnostics after John were Ignatius of Antioch and Irenaeus of Lyons. Two centuries later, the divine identity of Christ was disputed by the famous Alexandrian priest Arius. Athanasius, an Alexandrian deacon who later became the 20th patriarch of Alexandria, responded to the erroneous teachings of Arius. It was because of Arius that the emperor Constantine convened the first ecumenical council in Nicaea to settle the dispute. Nicene Orthodoxy insists on the divinity of Christ and His consubstantiality with the Father. It also insisted that the same Son of God became flesh in truth. Athanasius based his responses on his understanding of salvation. If Christ saves us, then He must be God because only God can save. If He is coming to save humans, then He must become human.

This left some with confusion as to how divinity and humanity were united in Christ. As a result, they began speculating how this unity would have taken place. Two famous figures of early Christianity are associated with false interpretations: Apollinaris, a bishop, and Nestorius, a patriarch. Apollinaris compromised the humanity of Christ when he taught that Christ had no rational soul and that such soul was replaced with the Logos. Athanasius did not live long enough to eliminate the impact of this heresy neither were his efforts in Nicaea and its aftermath conclusive. It was three Cappadocian men who kept the light of orthodoxy luminous, namely Basil the Great, his brother Gregory of Nyssa, and their friend Gregory of Nazianzus. Together, they defended three important elements of Christian theology: the integrity of the humanity of Christ, a theological formulation of the unity and diversity within the Trinity, and the divinity of the Holy Spirit. The last two elements will be covered in the section on the Trinity. For now, we will revert our attention to the first element pertaining to the humanity of Christ. Gregory of Nazianzus known as the Theologian coined his famous statement, "This which is not assumed is not healed."[2] In other words, the humanity of Christ consisted of everything a human being is in order to heal all that is human through the Incarnation. This came to be approved and universalized by the Church in the Council of Constantinople

Nestorius was a patriarch of Constantinople who deemed it unfit to call the Virgin Mary *Theotokos* (God bearer) and preferred to title her *Christotokos* (Christ bearer) or *anthropotokos* (man bearer). While it seems at first glance to be a controversy about Mary, it really was a controversy about who Christ is. Mary can only give birth to someone not something. As such, the Orthodox saw that she gave birth to the incarnate Word. Nestorius drew a distinction claiming there is a son of God born of the Father before all ages and a son of Mary born of her in time. These two sons are united in an external manner according to dignity. Whether Nestorius believed this or not is a matter of debate, but this is what the heresy that came to be associated with his name entailed. Cyril of Alexandria, the 24th patriarch of Alexandria, opposed Nestorius and exchanged letters with him hoping to persuade him of his errors. When the situation deteriorated further, Emperor Theodosius convened yet another ecumenical council in Ephesus. The Council upheld the orthodoxy of the doctrine of the Incarnation as coined by Cyril and condemned the formulation of Nestorianism to be heretical.

---

[2] Gregory of Nazianzus, *Letter to Cledonius the Priest Against Apollonarius*, 5.

Cyril described the Incarnation in the light of his famous phrase, "One nature of the Incarnate Word of God." Through this phrase, Cyril affirmed the oneness of Christ after the Incarnation. However, Cyril never denied the continuity and preservation of the existence of the divine and human natures in the One Christ. Cyril knew full well that this formulation did not appeal to the Church of Antioch which focused a lot more on the distinction of the divinity and humanity in Christ. Consequently, Cyril affirmed that one can distinguish between divinity and humanity in thought alone. Cyril describes the unity in his second Letter to Nestorius in the following terms,

> "We do not say that the nature of the Word was altered when he became flesh. Neither do we say that the Word was changed into a complete man of soul and body. We say rather that the Word by having united to himself hypostatically flesh animated by a rational soul, inexplicably and incomprehensibly became man... The difference of the natures is not destroyed through the union, but rather the divinity and humanity formed for us one Lord Jesus Christ and one Son through the incomprehensible and ineffable combination to a unity."[3]

It seems that the controversy was settled but in fact it was really beginning. Cyril died in 444 CE and was succeeded by Dioscorus, his disciple and deacon. He was a zealous man committed to the Cyrillian cause. He upheld the

---

[3] Cyril of Alexandria, *Letters: 1-50* (Washington DC: The Catholic University of America Press, 2007), 39.

same Christological understanding of Cyril which entailed that Christ was one nature and one hypostasis composed of full divinity and full humanity without mingling, confusion, or alteration. Divinity does not become humanity neither does humanity become divinity. Rather, the two are united in a manner that makes it impossible for us to divide the two natures after the union while equally making it impossible to deny the reality of the elements, divinity and humanity, from which the One Christ is composed.

A Constantinopolitan Archimandrite named Eutyches began spreading a heretical view that Christ was only divine; the divinity in its greatness must have swallowed up the humanity. This was not accepted by the bishop of Constantinople, Flavian, who excommunicated him. Eutyches protested his excommunication by appealing to Dioscorus. When Eutyches was examined by Dioscorus, the former produced an Orthodox confession of faith which compelled Dioscorus to think that Flavian was opposing the newly written Orthodox confession of Eutyches and thus excommunicated Flavian in the second council of Ephesus in 449 CE. To settle the dispute, yet another council was convened in Chalcedon in 451 CE at the call of Emperor Marcian. The council ended up siding with Flavian and his supporter Leo of Rome. Terminological disagreements and the stern measures of the council against Dioscorus made it difficult for Alexandrians, many Antiochians, and many residents of Jerusalem to accept the authority of the council. The fact the council invited and rehabilitated men such as Theodoret and Ibas, two crypto-Nestorian men who vehemently attacked Cyril, topped off the bitter taste in the mouths of Copts and Syrians toward Chalcedon. Ambiguities in the definition of faith and the Tome of Leo put forward by the council made it virtually impossible for non-Chalcedonians to accept the council due to fear of it leaving lots of room for a Nestorian interpretation. In this manner, the Copts, Syrians, Armenians, and Ethiopians came to be known as non-Chalcedonian because of their disapproval of the decisions and definitions of the council.

Today, both Eastern Chalcedonians and non-Chalcedonians affirm the unity of Christ, the reality, and fullness of His divinity and humanity. They also affirm that divinity and humanity preserved their faculties of will and activity, yet all is done in unity of hypostasis. Christ acts as One person but in acting He reflects the actions appropriate to His divine and human elements simultaneously. An example to illustrate the activities of Christ is given by Severus of Antioch when he describes Christ walking on water. Walking is a human activity. But walking on water is definitely above the capabilities of humanity and rather reflects His divine authority over nature. We cannot however divide this action into two. Regarding the wills, Severus writes,

> "He is indeed one from two, from divinity and humanity, one person and hypostasis, the one nature of the Logos, became flesh and perfect human being. For this reason, he also displays two wills in salvific suffering, the one which requests, the other which is prepared, the one human, the other divine. As he voluntarily took upon himself

death in the flesh, which was able to take over suffering and dissolved the domination of death by killing it through immortality—which the resurrection had shown clearly to all—so in the flesh, whose fruit he could take over—it was indeed rationally animated—he voluntarily took upon himself the passion of fear and weakness and uttered words of request, in order through the divine courage to destroy the power of that fear and to give courage to the whole of humanity, for he became after the first Adam the second beginning of our race."[4]

Thus, we can speak of two wills that are united and not opposed to one another. Admittedly, some Oriental Orthodox fathers occasionally speak of one will in Christ but this one will is composite as it is fully divine and fully human not merely divine. One may say that Christ wills as one person but in willing, He displays the divine and human wills—both of which have much in common as the latter is made in the image of the former. The harmony between the wills has its root in Christ being fully divine and fully human and as such, He did not have to deliberate or think whether an act is good or evil being all-knowing. Severus writes,

"With respect to Him (the new Adam) the prophet Isaiah says: 'Before he knows or chooses evil, he will choose good.' For before the child recognizes good or evil, he spurns evil in order to choose good…But because the Emmanuel is by nature also

---

[4] Severus of Antioch in Cyril Hovorun, *Will, Action, and Freedom: Christological Controversies in the Seventh Century* (Leiden: Brill Academic Publishers, 2008), 26.

God and goodness itself, although he has become a child according to the *eikonomia*, he did not await the time of the distinction; on the contrary, from the time of swaddling clothes, before he came to an age of distinguishing between good and evil, on the one side he spurned evil and did not listen to it, and on the other he chose good."[5]

This unity Severus insists on echoes the communication of properties of divinity and humanity Cyril insisted on when he said,

"[T]he Word appropriated the affairs of his own flesh because it is his body, no one else's. And He communicates, as to his own flesh, the operation of his own divine powers."[6]

The activities performed by the Incarnate Word are ascribed to His Person rather than to divinity or humanity separately. As the Ethiopian text *Haymanota Abaw* puts it,

"When you see Christ getting hungry, getting thirsty, sleeping and being crucified, do not attribute this to His humanity; when you see Him healing the sick, creating eyes, multiplying loaves of bread, rebuking the storm, do not say that these are God befitting. Do not attribute the higher deeds to His divinity and the lowly ones to His humanity. All belong to the incarnate Word; all the divine and human deeds are attributes of the one Lord. Being

---

[5] Hovorun, *Action, Will, and Freedom*, 27.

[6] Cyril of Alexandria, *Scholia of the Incarnation* in John Anthony McGuckin, *Saint Cyril of Alexandria and the Christological Controversy*, (Yonkers: SVS Press 2010), 300–301.

one-united nature (mia-physis) and one hypostasis, the Lord performs both the divine and human deeds."[7]

The Oriental Orthodox fathers engaged in the Chalcedonian controversy such as Dioscorus, Timothy II, and Severus of Antioch were often echoed by the fathers of the Churches that were further from the controversy geographically like the Ethiopian Tawahedo Orthodox Church and historically like the Indian Orthodox Church. For example, Abba Giyorgis, a fifteenth century Ethiopian bishop and theologian, was committed to the Cyrillian and non-Chalcedonian Christology that he was dubbed "The Ethiopian Cyril." Modern Indian Orthodox theologians such as Fr. V. C. Samuel and Metropolitan Paulos Gregorios were no less committed to the Oriental Orthodox confession of Christ as the "One Incarnate nature of God the Word" who is consubstantial with the Father according to His divinity and consubstantial with us according to His humanity. The Armenian Church, though it did not take part in the Council of Chalcedon, was committed to the one nature Christology, safeguarded in her various liturgical texts and the local councils that affirmed her faith in the Cyrillian Christology of the Oriental Orthodox Churches.

Now the question is: why does all of this matter? If all we said above about Christ is simply a set of facts with no practical implication in our lives, then Christianity is a mere philosophy under the direction of Jewish man named Jesus of

---

[7] *Hymanota Abaw* in Mebratu Kiros Gebru, *Miaphysite Christology: An Ethiopian Perspective*, (Piscataway: Gorgias Press 2010), 71.

Nazareth. However, if the coming of Christ has implications in our lives, then He is everything He claimed Himself to be (i.e., Messiah, King, High Priest, Mediator, Savior, God, and man).

The fathers unanimously believe that humanity is in need of salvation and redemption from sin, death, and the dominion of darkness. Therefore, the coming of Christ allowed the divine light of God to penetrate our dark cosmos, as John the Evangelist puts it, "the light shone in the darkness" (John 1:5). In the Incarnation, there is a descent and ascent; a descent of Christ as divine being into our world becoming one of us and an ascent of our humanity in Christ to sit at the right hand of the Father. One of the Trinity became one of us that we may have fellowship and communion with the Trinity. Our salvation is founded on the union of divinity and humanity in Christ which redeems the condition of separation from God which we suffered. It is necessary that Christ is God as God and only God can save. It is also necessary that Christ is human that in Him our humanity may be healed. Our human nature, human will, and human works are all healed by Christ who assumed everything that we are apart from sin. It is necessary that there be a natural and real union of divinity and humanity by which these two come together after having functioned independently since the fall of humanity.

It is impossible however to simply speak of salvation through the coming of Christ to earth alone. As Orthodox Christians, we firmly believe that the Incarnation is not merely the birth of Christ but is rather the entirety of His life on earth beginning in His conception and birth and continuing in flesh at the right hand of the Father. As such, we must know that our salvation is attained not only by the union of divinity and humanity but also through living the commandments of Christ. Furthermore, we understand salvation in relation to the mediation of the Cross. Upon the Cross, the Church becomes the bride of Christ which He acquired by His precious blood. His pierced side brought forth water and blood, signifying the baptism and Eucharist by which we are saved in Church. His stretched arms invited the whole world to be reconciled to one another regardless of race, ethnicity, or gender. All are to be reconciled in Him. In being hung between heaven and earth, He reconciles heaven and earth. Athanasius meditates on the cross and says that in the coming of Christ from heaven, He sanctified heaven; in walking on earth, He sanctified the earth; and in being hung between heaven and earth, He sanctified the air in between. The air which was once dominated by the prince of the air, Satan, is now reclaimed, sanctified and has become the place where Christ places His throne, the cross. He was hung on a wood reigning as King not only of the Jews as Pilate thought but rather as King of the whole world.

The Apostle Paul and Cyril of Alexandria emphasize our salvation being predicated upon being "in Christ." Paul writes, "Those who have been baptized into Christ have put on Christ" (Gal. 3:27). Commenting on this, Cyril insists that the day we are baptized, we become in a state of being "in Christ." This state makes us receive the graces of being born in Him, co-suffering with Him, co-rising with Him, and co-ascending with Him. We no longer see the events of his life as events from the past though they historically took place in the past. Rather, we see these events as our very own having been made members of Him. In His resurrection, we have our resurrection. In His ascension, we rejoice as our first fruit is now sitting at the right hand of the Father. Now we have a place in Him at the right hand of power. On this hope and this faith in Christ Jesus, we live, move, and have our being in His Church living the memory of His life through the Eucharistic Liturgy. More insight into the doctrine of salvation will come later as we discover Orthodox Christian anthropology.

Chapter 3
Tradition of the Church

The word tradition is a direct translation of the Greek word Paradosis which grants the meaning of handing down. The Tradition of the Church is the sum of the things which have been handed down to us from generation to generation. It is our duty to safeguard what we have received and hand it down to those who come after us through our life in the Church. The Tradition handed down to us is preserved in written texts, practiced rites, decisions of ecclesial councils, and oral teachings.

Scripture

> *"The Bible is not a precious book in the sense that it contains truths conceived and formulated by highly talented people of great genius. It is the Holy Book because the Holy God has revealed Himself in words and deeds recorded in the Bible by men in communion with Him and through His divine guidance and inspiration. His power is there in the Book. Through the use of the Bible in the worship of the Church we are not merely instructed intellectually in the Christian truth, but are touched by the power of God—the Breath of God."* [8]
>
> –*Catholicos Karekin I of Armenia*

+++

---

[8] Karekin II, *In Search of Spiritual Life: An Armenian Christian Miscellany*, (Antelias: Armenian Catholicosate of Cilicia, 1991), 178.

The first and foremost element of tradition is the Scriptures which can be defined as the texts the Church approved as an authentic written expression of a divinely inspired and guided human experience of the Divine. One may say Scripture is fully divine inasmuch as it reflects the divine identity of God who inspired them. One may also admit that it is fully human inasmuch as all expressions, philosophies, letters, and words that record the experience of the author were human. Divine inspiration in Christian thought is not synonymous with the classic Islamic conception of divine inspiration which really means divine dictation. Rather, we believe that Scriptures are the result of real divine-human synergy and experience.

In early Christianity, the word "scripture" was taken to refer to what we now call the Old Testament. These texts were seen as authoritative by Jews and Christians alike. Jews of the first century were more concerned with the five books of Moses which together form the Torah by which Jews lived. Christians, however, gave the prophets and wisdom literature more attention due to the fact these books point to Christ, the One of whom Moses and the prophets spoke.

After the ascension of Christ, disciples began to pass away and the need for written memoirs of the life of Christ arose. Traditionally, Mark wrote the first account of the life of Jesus followed by Matthew and Luke around the same time until lastly, we come to John who wrote his account toward the end of the first century if not beginning of the second. Even before these accounts of the life of Jesus were written, the apostles were establishing Christian communities celebrating the Eucharist combined with readings from the Old Testament. They were also receiving letters from the apostles such as Paul, Peter, John, Jude, and James. Some of their letters were preserved for us in the list of New Testament books which all Oriental Orthodox Christians uphold as sacred scriptures together with the Old Testament.

The list of books of the Old Testament was debated in the early Church between Jerome and Augustine. Jerome held the opinion that Christians needed not to consider any books as authoritative scriptures other than those which the Jews deem as such. Augustine saw books written in Greek such as Maccabees and Tobit to be equally authoritative. Augustine's rationale was that these writings reflected the dealings of God with the people of Israel between the times of the Minor Prophets and the coming of Christ. The opinion of Augustine prevailed in the universal Church until the protestant reformation which followed the opinion of Jerome.

In Oriental Orthodoxy, we do not have a strict list of books that are scriptural. There are books we are certain are apocryphal and heretical. However, we have an openness to diversity within the lists we consider canonical. The Ethiopian Church includes books such as Enoch, Teachings of the Apostles, and the Epistles of Clement of Rome as part of their canon of scripture. Copts have an additional Psalm to the 150 Psalms rendering the number 151 Psalms. Syrians add four Psalms to the 151 Psalms. Armenians historically added an additional epistle of Paul known as 3rd Corinthians. This did not cause any disputes among the Oriental Orthodox Churches because of awareness that even Church fathers held differing views as to what books constitute scriptures and which do not. Augustine and Jerome disagreed as I related earlier. Athanasius would not include Esther in his list of Old Testament books as he could not conceive of it being canonical scripture despite lack of any mention of the name of God.

The Orthodox Church canonized the list of the books from the Old and New Testament which are considered as authoritative texts revealing what humanity has known about God as He revealed Himself to it. Though the lists differ, the substance of the texts considered as sacred is one and the same. Furthermore, we believe that these books the Church canonized as scriptural are considered divinely inspired, or more precisely God breathed. The Scripture being the Word of God is interpreted in the light of the Incarnate Word of God, Jesus Christ Himself. The Scripture being divinely inspired by the Holy Spirit as we recite in the Creed is to be read with the guidance of the Spirit. Therefore, the Church, as the body of Christ and the dwelling place of the Spirit, fully reserves the right to interpret all the texts in the Bible. The Church was aware of this vocation since the beginning of her birth that many of the bishops, as spokesmen of the Church, have composed lengthy commentaries on Scripture. They often agreed and occasionally disagreed. With regard to dogma, they did not disagree on substance even though they would seldom differ in the way they formulate a dogma while maintaining the one substance of the faith. There was no disagreement in confessing a triune God or the divinity of Christ. However, there was an openness for variety of opinions on matters that are undogmatic. For example, church fathers approached eschatology, the study of the end of times, differently and drew different conclusions. Regarding scriptures, the fathers of the Church had various methods of approaching the scriptural texts (literal, typological, allegorical, etc.).

Scholars suggest that there were two main schools of interpretation: the school of Alexandria and the school of Antioch. Each school had its unique features, methods and styles by which it interpreted the sacred texts of the divinely inspired scriptures. The differences between the schools have often been overly exaggerated. The school of Alexandria had theological attributes that shaped its way of providing an exegesis for scripture. Fr. Tadros Malaty, a Coptic Orthodox priest and scholar, summarizes these characteristics in his book *The School of Alexandria Before Origen*: (1) Centrality of Deification to theology, (2) Oneness of life, (3) Soteriological Theology, (4) Repentance, (5) Theological terms from Greek philosophy, (6) Lack of definitions of theological terminology, and (7) Ecumenical Spirit.[9] Deification was confessed by the school of Alexandria since the time of Clement of Alexandria and Origen of Alexandria until it was inherited and formulated in relation to the Incarnation in the writings of Athanasius of

---

[9] Tadros Malaty, *The School of Alexandria, Book One: Before Origen*, (Sydney: Pope Shenouda III Coptic Theological College, 1995), 15–29.

Alexandria. Solutions for most theological issues were based on the centrality of our salvation i.e., soteriology. The school highly depended on Greek philosophy though it did not spend a lot of time defining what each term meant. The students lived in oneness of life with real fellowship and a repentant life in which their academic schooling was inseparable from their spirituality. Students from all churches were equally welcome to become part of the school of Alexandria. This atmosphere created deep richness from which the Alexandrian style of interpretation emerged.

Origen of Alexandria was among the pioneers of the allegorical method of biblical interpretation. However, one cannot limit his interpretation of scripture to the allegorical method. In a document called *Hexapla*, Origen created six columns in which he compared the Hebrew texts with the Greek translations of the Old Testament and recorded his notes. He is said to have visited sites where scriptural events would take place in order for him to cultivate a better understanding of the text. Writings attributed to Origen were later the cause of his excommunication. However, he is still considered a scholar upon whom pillars of the Church such as Gregory the Wonderworker, Basil of Caesarea, Gregory of Nyssa, and Gregory Nazianzus have depended. Cyril of Alexandria would have been remembered for his commentaries on Scripture that resemble the spirit of the school of Alexandria in every way if it were not for the Nestorian controversy that made him memorable for his Christological triumph instead of his exegetical expertise.

Some scholars of the modern era suggest that the school of Antioch arose to counter the allegorical method of Alexandria. More recent scholarship claim that this is an exaggeration of the differences between the two schools. The school of Antioch certainly paid more attention to the literal, historical, and moralistic elements of the scriptural texts than the school of Alexandria. This is not to suggest that the school of Alexandria ignored such elements of interpretation, but they certainly were not the point of emphasis. The school of Antioch, unlike the school of Alexandria, paid a lot of attention to the interpretation of theological terms and rationalizing texts in a coherent and logical way. Theodore of Mopsuestia, Theodoret of Cyrus, and John Chrysostom were among the Christian thinkers who brought fame to the school of Antioch. However, the dangers of over rationalizing scripture left Theodore and Theodoret anathematized and excommunicated. Chrysostom's moralistic interpretation of scripture seen in his homilies however made him carved in the memory of the Church as the greatest orator of the Church of Constantinople. The differences, theological and political, between the schools of Alexandria and Antioch inflated and deflated throughout history. By the fifth century, the differences of interpretation of theological texts would leave the Church with a Christological controversy that left the Church in schism since 451 CE.

Liturgical texts

What we pray in the Liturgy is the dogma of the Church as it is lived by the people. What we pray is what we believe and what we believe is what we live. Liturgy is the translation of our beliefs into life. The Oriental Orthodox Churches are rich with a diverse heritage of liturgical texts. Our unity is in our faith in the Liturgy and its efficacy and not in the uniformity of the Liturgies we pray.

Copts pray the Liturgies of Basil, Gregory the Theologian, and Cyril of Alexandria. It is believed that there used to be tens of other liturgies that were often prayed such as the Liturgy of Severus of Antioch and the Liturgy of Serapion. The Coptic synod, under the guidance of the late His Holiness Pope Shenouda III, restricted the liturgies to be prayed to just those attributed to Basil, Gregory the Theologian, and Cyril of Alexandria.

The Tawahedo Orthodox Churches of Ethiopia and Eritrea pray numerous liturgies namely the *anaphoras* of the Apostles, the Lord, John the Son of Thunder, St. Mary, the Three Hundred, Athanasius, Basil, Gregory of Nyssa, Epiphanius, John Chrysostom, Cyril, Jacob of Serug, Dioscorus, and Gregory II the Wonderworker.

The Syriac Orthodox Church pray liturgies attributed to James, Mark, Peter, Twelve Apostles, Xystus, Julius, John Chrysostom, Cyril, Jacob of Serug, Philoxenus of Mabbug, Severus of Antioch, and Mar Bar Salibi.

The Armenian Apostolic Church prays a liturgy attributed to Athanasius of Alexandria.

These liturgies together form the rich liturgical tradition of the Oriental Orthodox Church which encompasses Eastern and Western elements of Liturgizing. The Coptic, Syrian, and Ethiopian Churches represent the Eastern side of Oriental Orthodoxy whereas the Armenian Church possesses elements of the East and West. Among the western characteristics of the Armenian liturgy are the use of the organ, use of unleavened bread for the Eucharist, and most of its jurisdictions following the Gregorian calendar.

Ecumenical Councils

Many attempt to romanticize the place of the ecumenical councils of the Church, granting it the status of highest authority in Church. Indeed, the ecumenical councils hold a high place in Church because of their formulations of Christian doctrines. However, we must not lose sight of why the councils were convened. Church fathers did not simply decide to gather and formulate Christian doctrines. Rather, councils were convened to respond to heresies. To use an analogy, the councils acted like a cast. When one breaks his arm, they need a cast. One who is whole does not need a cast. Similarly, the heresies spreading were breaking the peace of the Church. The councils came about to restore such peace although it was not always successful in such endeavor. This is clear in the writings and lives of the saints who lived through these times. Athanasius had to flee his see five times because the decisions of Nicaea were not conclusive in as much as they did not put an end to Arianism and required more nuance. Gregory of Nazianzus left the Council of

Constantinople in sorrow and pain at the lukewarm approach the bishops had toward the doctrine of the Spirit. Cyril of Alexandria was imprisoned in the events leading up to Ephesus. The complex political, terminological, and theological matrix of the Council of Chalcedon caused a schism between Chalcedonians and non-Chalcedonians which sadly persists to this day.

However, one ought to be thankful for the sweat and blood which our fathers shed for the sake of preserving the faith of the Church through ecumenical councils. The first two ecumenical councils provide us with the Nicene-Constantinopolitan Creed which we recite in liturgies to this day. The third ecumenical council gives us an appropriate theological language through which we can describe the economy and manner of the Incarnation. Each Oriental Orthodox Church believes these three councils to be ecumenical though each Church has its local councils and synodal meetings.

Patristic Texts

The writings of apologetic fathers, desert fathers, fathers of the ecumenical councils, poets and theologians of the Church have been largely preserved in Greek, Syriac, Ga'ez, Coptic, and Armenian. We uphold most of the writings of the fathers who composed Christian writings prior to the council of Chalcedon as a common heritage we share with other Apostolic Christian Churches such as the Roman Catholic Church, the Eastern Orthodox Church, and the Assyrian Church of the East. The second and third centuries were illuminated by the writings of saints and scholars such as Ignatius of Antioch, Justin the Martyr, Clement of Rome, Clement of Alexandria, and Irenaeus of Lyons. The fourth and fifth centuries are the richest when it comes to patristic writings of saints such as Ephraim the Syrian, Athanasius of Alexandria, Basil the Great, Gregory the Theologian, Gregory of Nyssa, Gregory the Armenian (The illuminator), Cyril of Alexandria, John Chrysostom and Dioscorus of Alexandria. The sixth century was a time of theological debate where Severus of Antioch and Philoxenus of Mabbug stood out as the defenders of the Orthodox Christology of Cyril of Alexandria. Simultaneously, a Syriac poet and a vigorous ascetic named Jacob of Serug chose to stay away from the controversy and emerged as a spiritual successor of Ephraim the Syrian. Just as Ephraim of Syria was called the harp of the Spirit, likewise Jacob of Serug came to be known as the flute of the Spirit. Ethiopia not being involved, at least initially, in the Chalcedonian controversy had Yared, the great composer of the hymns of the Tawahedo tradition. The tenth century marked the emergence of the Armenian saint, theologian, and poet Gregory of Narek. His illustrious poems made Pope Francis of Rome consider him a doctor of the Catholic Church despite him not being in communion with the Church of Rome. Twelfth-century Syriac Orthodoxy was blessed with Mor Dionysius Bar Saliba who wrote commentaries on scripture and authored the last anaphora of the Syriac Orthodox Church. Bulus Al-Bushi was a Coptic saint, homilist, and commentator who left the Coptic Church with a heritage reflecting the rich patristic heritage of Alexandria in the thirteenth century. In Syria, Bar Hebraeus from the thirteenth century was a prolific author of different fields of knowledge such as philosophy, poetry, language, history, and theology. Many of the fathers were bishops who were invested with the grace of the Spirit and have enjoyed the apostolic continuity and succession, meaning that they could trace their line of bishops back to one of the Apostles. Succession is a fundamental element of tradition as it is the mode of transmitting and protecting correct and Orthodox teachings. The fathers were clear in dictating that a valid Church with valid sacraments and a valid Eucharist are only possible with a bishop who traces his roots back to the apostles of Christ. A rightful bishop as such is one who, having received apostolic succession, brings forth the word of God spoken through his teachings received from the apostles and brings forth the Word of God in an edible form through the Eucharist.

What theologians and bishops put in theological formulations the saints of the desert put in an applicable format comparable to the kerygma of the apostles. Luminous figures such as Anthony, Macarious, Amoun, Agathon, Poemen, Shenouda the Archimandrite, Thekla Haymanout, Sarah, and Syncletica of Alexandria and many other ascetics had their homilies recorded in written texts for the edification of monks and laity alike. The writings of the ascetics light the path of Christian life working out our salvation in fear and trembling. The writings of the theologians answer us as to why we are on the path of Christian life.

Iconography

The Church, being a mother, attends to the needs of all her children, the educated and the illiterate alike. To those who could not read the texts of the fathers I mentioned earlier, the church provided education through images. The walls of churches in Egypt, Syria, Armenia, and Ethiopia bear witness of the iconographic legacy of these churches. Though there was never a major iconoclastic controversy like that of the Eastern Orthodox Church of Byzantium, the Oriental Orthodox communion was always attached to iconography in worship and liturgy. Even the Syriac Church, which does not use icons in its system of liturgical worship, has countless manuscripts with holy images of the life of Christ, lives of saints, and portraits of holy men. Furthermore, the Syriac Orthodox Church has a unique prayer for the blessing of an icon made for personal use. In the Coptic Orthodox Church, Metropolitan Mikhail of Damietta created a Bible with images for the education and edification of his simple congregants. Not much about his life is preserved but the Copts continue to have a copy of the Bible he wrote through images.

In Coptic and Ethiopian Churches, the icons of Christ, the Theotokos, angels, and saints create an ethos that reminds the believers of the Church being a meeting place where heaven and earth are no longer two separate realities but rather one reality in which we and the communion of the departed saints realize our unity as members of the one body of Christ.

Western influence has unfortunately permeated many Oriental Orthodox parishes, especially Coptic Orthodox parishes, causing many members to prefer the realism of western art to the abstraction of Orthodox icons. Many churches are now filled with western images that in no way reflect the theology or ethos of Orthodox icons. In the twentieth century, Dr. Isaac Fanous from the Coptic Orthodox Church received education in iconography at the hands of Vladimir Lossky and Leonid Ouspensky and returned to Egypt with the mission of reviving Coptic iconography. It is thanks to him that today more Coptic parishes are implementing the use of Coptic icons rather than western images. It must be noted however that throughout the years, the Coptic Church has used different styles of iconography which were often the work of Egyptians, Armenians, and Byzantines. This created a diversity of styles within ancient Egyptian iconography which reflected the cosmopolitan identity of ancient Egypt.

In all, iconography is a part of the life of all Oriental Orthodox communities without which the Church would be missing a great element of her theology and spirituality. If Christ became man (material flesh and blood), then we have every reason to depict images of Him, His Mother, angels, and saints through material wood, colors, and frescos. In no way do we fear the use of images being confused with idolatry. Even when God commanded the Israelites to create no idols or graven images, God also commanded them to create a house for Him that encompassed an illustrious arc of the covenant with two cherub statues over it among many other carved and painted elements of decoration used to beautify and inform the liturgical lives of the Israelites. In this light, Orthodox Christians use icons as a tool for prayer and communication of the divine and heavenly presence in our earthly realm.

Chapter 4

The Holy Trinity

In chapter two, we covered who Jesus Christ is and in chapter three, how we come to know Him through the living tradition of the Church. The coming of Christ revealed the triune reality of the divine. In this chapter, I will attempt to illustrate what the Oriental Orthodox Churches believe about God and how they articulate such beliefs.

How to Speak about God?

There are two ways to speak about or describe God: the cataphatic and apophatic. The cataphatic way affirms the realities we know about God i.e., God is good, loving, merciful, etc. The apophatic way refers to the awareness of what God is not i.e., God is ineffable, indescribable, etc. These ways of speaking about God remind us that God is beyond all forms of speech. The greatest way of speaking about God is to stand before Him in silence with your heart speaking to Him. However, given our reality as rational beings, we need to converse about and with God. In doing so, we make cataphatic statements, but we know that they are mere words that do not limit who He is but simply tell us what we can know about Him through human language. Apophatic statements are made to engrave the fact He is beyond all knowledge, speech, and conception.

Jesus' words about Himself, His Father, the Spirit, and the relationship between the three persons of the Trinity are recorded in the four accounts of the Gospel, especially that of John. These words are the primary source of all we know about the Trinity. The Old Testament and the rest of the New Testament bear witness of the triune reality of God as well.

The One and the Three

After countless theological quarrels in the fourth century, the doctrine of the Trinity was formulated in the Creed and the writings of the fathers who opposed Arianism and Pneumatomachians (those who believed the Spirit to be counted with the angels rather than *homousious* or of one essence with the Father and the Son). The New Testament makes it clear that Christ is divine, and the book of Acts shows the Spirit causing real change in the apostles and all Christians which made them believe Him to be divine. It was difficult however for many early Christians to formulate their belief in the oneness of God reconciled with their belief in the divinity of Christ and the Spirit.

After the Nicene and Constantinopolitan councils, the Church formulated the doctrine of the Trinity affirming the oneness of the substance (or *ousia*) of God and the diversity of the three persons (or hypostases) who are distinct but not separated. The three are united in the bond of love and oneness of substance, will, and activity. The oneness is not compromised by the multiplicity of persons neither is the diversity of persons compromised by the unity.

This fundamental doctrine of Orthodox Christianity has brought the Church much pain and turmoil. The pagans and polytheists deemed them insane for believing in one God whereas the Jews deemed them heretical for believing in three persons in the Godhead. Islamists would later, like Jews, persecute Christians on grounds of association with polytheism. For this reason, Oriental Orthodox communions such as the Coptic, Ethiopian, and Syriac Churches add the phrase "One God" at the end of the sign of the Cross. This addition is not found in other Churches such as the Armenian Apostolic Church, Chalcedonian Orthodox Church, or Roman Catholic Church who simply say, "In the name of the Father, the Son and the Holy Spirit. Amen."

Begotten-ness and Procession

As Orthodox Christians, we often recite the Creed which describes the relationship of the Son as begotten of the Father and the relationship of the Spirit as proceeding from the Father. These words seem ambiguous to most of us as they are not everyday words. Church fathers such as Gregory of Nazianzus and Cyril of Alexandria after him offer a famous analogy by which we can understand the difference between these two words:

> Adam, Eve and Seth are three persons. All three belong to the same category of humanity. They all relate to each other differently. Adam is the source of both Eve and Seth. Seth is begotten of Adam whereas Eve proceeds from His side. Undoubtedly, this analogy is by no means perfect at all. Adam, Eve and Seth did not all exist at the same time.

They certainly did not share the same will or activities.[10]

In the case of human beings, we are all persons belonging to the same category of humanity. However, we are separated by differing wills, our existence at different times, and in different spatial locations. In the case of God, all three persons have their existence outside time and space and thus are not separated by such factors. All three share the same will and same activity. As Athanasius and Cyril put it, "The Father does all things by the Son in the Holy Spirit."[11] This descriptive formula certainly does not correspond to our fallen human reality.

The Holy Spirit

Just as some doubted the oneness of the Father and the Son in essence, others have doubted the oneness of the Spirit with the Father and the Son. Those came to be known as Pneumatomachians (opposers of the Spirit). In combating them, Athanasius wrote four letters to Bishop Serapion where he illustrated how the Spirit belongs to the same divinity of the Father and the Son. The Cappadocians followed his footsteps and wrote illustrious discourses and gave prolific orations describing the relationship of the Spirit to the Father and the Son. Basil the Great for example wrote

---

[10] See Gregory of Nazianzus, *Fifth Theological Oration: On the Holy Spirit*, *Oration 31*.10 and Cyril of Alexandria, *Dialogues on the Trinity*.

[11] Cyril of Alexandria, *Commentary on John (Vol. 2)*, Joel C. Elowsky (ed.), David R. Maxwell (trans.), *Ancient Christian Texts: Cyril of Alexandria's Commentary on the Gospel of John*, (Downers Grove: InterVarsity Press, 2015), 212.

a discourse on the Holy Spirit where he made use of tradition, rhetoric, and liturgical texts to leave no room for any doubt of the Spirit being the Lord equal with the Son and the Father though he refrained from calling the Spirit God. However, no one was bolder than Gregory the Theologian who unapologetically said that the Holy Spirit is God. Gregory the Theologian describes the activity of the Spirit in one of his orations,

> "From the Spirit comes our rebirth, from rebirth comes a new creating, from new creating a recognition of the worth of him who effected it… The Spirit it is who created and creates anew through baptism and resurrection. The Spirit it is who knows all things, who teaches all things, who blows where, and as strongly as, he wills, who leads, speaks, sends out, separates, who is vexed and tempted. He reveals, illumines, gives life—or, rather, is absolutely Light and Life. He makes us his temple, he deifies, he makes us complete, and he initiates us in such a way that he both precedes baptism and is wanted after it. All that God actively performs, he performs. Divided in fiery tongues, he distributes graces, makes Apostles, prophets, evangelists, pastors, and teachers."[12]

As per the words of Philoxenus of Mabbug, we believe that the Spirit never departs the believer who partakes of Him through baptism and chrismation. Even when we sin,

---

[12] Gregory of Nazianzus, *On God and Christ: The Five Theological Orations and Two Letters to Cledonius* (Yonkers: SVS Press, 2002), 139–40.

the Spirit is the One who draws us to repent and receive divine forgiveness. As Philoxenus puts it,

> "If it were true that the Spirit immediately departs the sinner which is the opinion of the ignorant who claim that they cannot partake of the sacrament. If the sinner is not permitted to partake of the sacrament, then who can? What becomes of the words 'This is my Body... This is my Blood of the covenant shed for many for the remission of sins?'"[13]

The main role of the Spirit is to remind us of the things which Christ spoke not in the abstract sense of remembering but rather in the same sacramental sense in which we offer the Eucharist in "memory" of the economy of Christ. The Spirit does not remind us externally but rather imprints the life and work of Christ within us. The Spirit unites the believers through His work in the Church, yet He gives each person according to their needs thus safeguarding the diversity of the members of the body of Christ. Through the Spirit, the Church possess the *chrism* by which it flourishes and grows in knowledge of Christ and the Father, which is eternal life. This knowledge provided by the chrism of the Spirit is communicated through the sacramental life of the Church. Through the Spirit present in the sacraments, we come to be with Christ and in Christ and have the grace of adoption by which we call God, "Abba Father" (Romans 8:15). We come to know the Father through the revelation of the Son by the power, grace, communion, and fellowship

---

[13] Nancy Magdy, *The Dwelling of the Spirit by Philoxenos of Mabbug*, (Alexandria: St George Church Sporting), 25-26.

with the Holy Spirit ever present in the Church. More on the work of the Spirit in the human being and in the Church is covered in subsequent chapters.

Unity and Diversity

In the previous chapter, I mentioned that if all that we learn about Christ has no practical implications in our lives, then it is a mere obsolete philosophical system. The same applies to the doctrine of the Holy Trinity.

The Trinity provides us an icon with what we ought to become. We are diverse in terms of our ethnicity, gender, status, and so on. However, we can become one when we unite our differing wills with the divine will by desiring the salvation of all. At such point, humanity is able to imitate the Trinity having formed a unity within our diversity. Such unity is not to be confused with uniformity. Uniformity is when all are the same and all distinctions are removed. This can never create a unity. Unity is when those who are distinct and continue to be so create a single whole. An analogy that would help us understand this is that of a puzzle. If the pieces of the puzzle are identical, they could never form a coherent image. However, when they are different from one another, they are able to form the intended image. Therefore, we are not united despite our diversity but rather we are united because of it. In such manner, Christians are supposed to create bonds that keep this trinitarian understanding of unity and diversity in mind. In a fallen world filled with a plethora of ideologies, this can be nearly impossible. The Church is the exception to this rule as it is where the reality of human diversity becomes united in the body of Christ with the power of the Spirit.

Chapter 5

The Church of Christ

"There came out from His side water and blood. Beloved, do not pass this mystery by without a thought. For I have still another mystical explanation to give. I said that there was a symbol of baptism and the mysteries in that blood and water. It is from both of these that the church is sprung through the bath of regeneration and the renewal of the Holy Spirit (Tit 3:5), through baptism and the mysteries. But the symbols of baptism and the mysteries come from the side of Christ. It is from His side, therefore, that Christ formed the Church, just as He formed Eve from the side of Adam... Just as at that time God took the rib of Adam and formed a woman, so Christ gave us blood and water from His side and formed the Church. Just as when He took the rib from Adam when he was in deep sleep, so now He gave us the blood and water after His death, first water and then the blood... Have you seen how Christ unites to Himself His bride? Have you seen with what food He nurtures us all?"

- John Chrysostom, Baptismal Instructions 3.17[14]

+++

The Church drew the attention of prominent Christian figures in the early years of Christianity who tried to answer the questions:

---

[14] John Chrysostom in *Ancient Christian Writers: The Works of the Fathers in Translation* No. 31, Johannes Quasten and Walter J. Burghardt (eds.), (Westminster: The Newman Press, 1963), 62.

What is the Church? How is the Church related to Christ? How is the Church related to the Spirit? What is the communion of saints? What is the role of the bishop, priest and deacon? Paul was the first Christian author to identify the Church with the body of Christ. This should not come as a surprise given that Paul heard Christ identifying Himself with the Church Paul persecuted before his conversion. Jesus said, "Saul, why are you persecuting Me?" although Paul was persecuting the Church. Thus, Paul understood the fact Christ and the Church are inseparable the way the head and the body are. Ignatius of Antioch, a disciple of John the Evangelist according to tradition, was the first to identify the place of the Eucharist and the bishop within the Church. Justin the Martyr was the first to give a coherent account of how liturgies were performed in the early Church. The Nicene- Constantinopolitan Creed came to formulate its doctrine of the Church in the light of four characteristics: "One, Holy, Catholic, and Apostolic."

Oneness

The Church being an icon of the Trinity, ought to reflect elements of unity resembling the oneness of God and elements of diversity mimicking the multiplicity of persons (Father, Son, and Holy Spirit). The Church is also the body of Christ and thus it is always united to His divinity. Members of the Church are said to be one with God because they are united to Him through living the one faith, worshipping the One Lord and receiving the one baptism by which they put on the One Lord. The Oriental Orthodox

Churches reflect the icon of unity in diversity as Copts, Syrians, Ethiopians, and Armenians share the one faith and one Eucharist, yet they do not pray the same liturgies nor speak the same languages nor live in the same culture or geographical locations. Thus, they invite comparison with Irenaeus' understanding of the Church,

> "The Church, though dispersed throughout the world... having received [this faith from the Apostles]... as if occupying but one house, carefully preserves it. She also believes these points [of doctrine] just as if she had but one soul and one and the same heart, and she proclaims them, and teaches them and hands them down with perfect harmony as if she possessed only one mouth. For, although the languages of the world are dissimilar, yet the import of the tradition is one and the same. For the Churches which have been planted in Germany do not believe or hand down anything different, nor do those in Spain, nor those in Gaul, nor those in the East, nor those in Egypt, nor those in Libya, nor those which have been established in the central regions of the world."[15]

The same ideas are echoed by Cyril of Alexandria, in his work *Worship in Spirit and Truth*,

> "The fullness of the Churches in the whole world... do not differ in their views nor are at odds in their beliefs, but are one in the Spirit. It is as if they were tied together to form one entity, like that which is in Christ, by faith. For in all the churches

---

[15] Irenaeus of Lyons, *Against the Heresies*, 1.10.

everywhere the Lord is but one, faith is but one, baptism is but one."[16]

Holiness

The holiness of the Church is derived first and foremost from Christ to whom the Church is united as bride together with the Holy Spirit who indwells the Church. The Holy Spirit sanctifies the members through the sacramental life of the Church ensuring that we attain a holy life. Holiness is healing from sin and passions[17] through the Church, the hospital in which sinners receive healing and become saints. This is seen most vividly in the sacraments of baptism and the unction of the sick.

In the exorcism prayers preceding the baptism of a new member of the Church, the presbyter guides the new member or his parents if the new member is a child into looking westward to renounce Satan. Then they turn around to recite the Creed and reclaim themselves to the family of God. This turning of body is a reminder of repentance being a change of mind and direction. We turn away from the devil known in Greek as *diavolos*, literally meaning the one who divides. Then, we turn to recite the symbol of faith known in Greek as *symvolon*, literally meaning the one which unites or brings

---

[16] Cyril of Alexandria, *Worship in Spirit and Truth*, Article 9 in *Worship in Spirit and Truth*, George Awad Ibrahim (trans.) (Cairo: Orthodox Patristics Centre 2010), 376.

[17] In the writings of the fathers, the word for passions and pain is the same Greek word *Pathos*. The Desert fathers would always speak of ascetic practices as exercises that help us become healed of our sinful pains and passions.

together. The creed is known by this name because it brings together all the articles of faith that every member of the family of God ought to affirm and believe. Holiness in Orthodox Christianity is intimately linked to being wholly dedicated to God with an undivided heart.

The notion of holistic healing is also seen in the rite of the anointing of the sick. The prayers recited are never simply concerned with the health of the body but is concerned with our entire being. In this manner, the Church ensures that her own intrinsic holiness granted to her from God is dispensed to the members of Christ. The concept of healing is inseparable from making us holy. We aim toward

> "com[ing] to the unity of the faith and of the knowledge of the Son of God, to a perfect man, to the measure of the stature of the fullness of Christ; that we should no longer be children, tossed to and fro and carried about with every wind of doctrine, by the trickery of men, in the cunning craftiness of deceitful plotting, but, speaking the truth in love, may grow up in all things into Him who is the head—Christ— from whom the whole body, joined and knit together by what every joint supplies, according to the effective working by which every part does its share, causes growth of the body for the edifying of itself in love."
>
> Ephesians 4: 13-16

Catholicity

We are often taught that the word Catholic means universal. While that is true, it is certainly incomplete. The word Catholic also implies bringing together. The Church aims to bring all into the fold of Christ. Furthermore, catholicity implies a sense of fullness or wholeness. The Church is ultimately Christ, who is all in all (Col. 3:11), given to the believers in the grace of the sacraments. We also know that Christ is "the Truth." Therefore, if the Church participates in the universal Truth, Christ Himself, then the Church ought to be universal. The Church derives her universality from Christ's universality and the universality of the revelation He brought to the world—namely that the Father loved the world, gave up His only begotten Son that those who believe may not perish but live unto life eternal in fellowship with the Holy Spirit.

Seas and mountains separate the fathers from one another, but distance does not come in the way of their agreement for they all relied on the one grace of the Holy Spirit. The catholicity of the Church is present and safeguarded by the fullness of the Church that is present in every local parish where the Eucharist is headed by the bishop or his representative from the presbyters.

Apostolicity

Catholicity and apostolicity are almost two sides of the same coin: if Catholicity is concerned with the universal reality of Christ as One who is and whose Church is beyond the boundaries of space, apostolicity is about the truth of Orthodoxy being beyond the boundaries of time. If Orthodoxy participates in Christ in whom there is no change or shadow of turning, then the faith and practice of

Orthodoxy ought to have no change or shadow of turning in its substance no matter how many centuries have passed since the ascension of Christ. This is attested to by the writings of early fathers who describe the life of the Church as early as the second century. Ignatius of Antioch who was devoured by beasts in the arena in Rome in 108 CE writes the following about the place of bishops and presbyters in the Church,

> "You must all follow the bishop as Jesus Christ follows the Father, and the presbytery as you would the apostles. Reverence the deacons as you would the command of God. Let no one do anything of concern to the Church without the bishop. Let that be considered a valid Eucharist which is celebrated by the bishop, or by one whom he appoints."[18]

A Christian philosopher named Justin the Martyr was martyred in 160 CE writes the following regarding the Divine Liturgy,

> "But we, after we have thus washed him who has been convinced and has assented to our teaching, bring him to the place where those who are called the brethren are assembled in order that we may offer hearty prayers in common for ourselves and for the baptized [illuminated] person, and for all others in every place, that we may be counted worthy, now that we have learned the truth, by our works also to be found good citizens and keepers of the commandments, so that we may be saved with an everlasting salvation. Having ended the

---

[18] Ignatius of Antioch, *Epistle to the Smyrnaeans*, 8.

prayers, we salute one another with a kiss. There is then brought to the president of the brethren bread and a cup of wine mixed with water; and he taking them, gives praise and glory to the Father of the universe, through the name of the Son and of the Holy Ghost, and offers thanks at considerable length for our being counted worthy to receive these things at His hands and when he has concluded the prayers and thanksgivings, all the people present express their assent by saying Amen... And when the president has given thanks, and all the people have expressed their assent, those who are called by us the deacons give to each of those present to partake of the bread and wine mixed with water over which the thanksgiving was pronounced and to those who are absent they carry away a portion."[19]

The Oriental Orthodox Churches continue to have the bishopric, presbytery, and diaconate to this day. The elements of the Liturgy Justin the Martyr describes in 160 CE differ in no way from what we do in our churches now. This continuity is safeguarded by the power of the Holy Spirit and apostolic succession through which bishops hand down to one another what they have received.

Christological Ecclesiology

Before creation, the Spirit of God was hovering over the face of the earth. The word hover in its Semitic roots give the meaning of embracing as Ephraim the Syrian and Basil

---

[19] Justin Martyr, *First Apology*, 65.

the Great teach us. When God created the world, He created Eden as to be a home for Adam and Eve. The word *Eden* means pleasure. Irenaeus of Lyons associates Eden with a virgin soil or virgin ground. When the Spirit of God embraced the virgin ground, *bios* or biological life came into being. After the creation of Adam, God creates Eve from the side of Adam. As Adam beheld Eve, he said, "a man shall leave his father and mother and be joined to his wife" (Genesis 2:24). Interestingly, no man in the Old Testament leaves his parents to marry a woman. Rebecca came to Isaac. Jacob and Moses flee from danger then get married, but they do not leave their parents for the purpose of getting married. When Adam and Eve are tempted by the serpent, Eve says "yes" to the serpent and "no" to God.

Before the coming of Christ, the Spirit hovered over the Virgin Mary that she brought forth *zoë* uncreated Life in human form, that is Christ Himself. Mary's "yes" to God undid the "yes" Eve said to the serpent. Christ's birth brought pleasure and goodwill in the hearts of humanity as the angels proclaimed, "Glory to God in the highest, and on earth peace and goodwill in men" (Luke 2:14). We no longer dwell in pleasurable Eden but rather the pleasure and joy of His dwelling within us. It is no longer a mere external experience but rather an internal one.

When Christ was crucified on the Cross, He was away from His Father's glory economically being on earth and away from His mother being hung on the cross and lifted up from the earth. At this point, He was joined to His bride, the Church, which He has acquired with His precious blood. Just as Eve came out of the side of Adam, the Church came from the side of Christ in the form of water and blood which signifies the baptism and eucharist by which we become members of His body. We should also note that the beginning of the path of Christ's passion and His resurrection took place in a garden just as the eating of the fruit took place in a garden.

Irenaeus of Lyons teaches that the work of Christ on earth was the recapitulation of humanity. The things Adam and Eve did Christ visited in a mystical way, reversed them, and renewed them. This is seen in the parallels between the events of creation and the events of the birth, suffering, and resurrection of Christ. It can also be seen in the triumph of Christ in the temptation on the Mount as Satan tempted Him with vainglory (power to fall without being hurt), the lust of the eyes (seeing the kingdoms of the world), and the lust of the flesh (turning stone into bread). These temptations echo the temptations with which Adam and Eve were tempted as the fruit offered them vainglory in becoming God like, lust of the eye as the fruit looked pleasing to the eyes, and the lust of the flesh inasmuch as it was a break of divinely appointed fast from the fruit. The good which we fail to do alone, God in Christ works with us, in us, and by us to accomplish. Christ, who has suffered being tempted, is able to aid those who are tempted (Hebrews 2:18). We are joined to Him, His suffering, and triumph through the sacramental life of the Church. This intimate reality is what gives the Church her Christological dimension by which she becomes not a mere representative of Christ but rather the body by which Christ is made present for the life of the world. On a personal level, we ought to have Christ be formed within us spiritually as He was formed in the Theotokos physically. This cannot be attained apart from the Church that is His body. In order to become members of His body, we must die with Him through baptism, eat His flesh and drink His blood, and resurrect unto the newness of life as new creation in the crucified and risen Christ. This unity with God is only attainable through the eucharistic unity by which He abides in us and us in Him.

Mariological Ecclesiology

The Church cannot be seen apart from motherhood. We can contemplate the feminine or motherly attributes of God in the Holy Spirit. We can certainly see motherly elements in Eve who brought forth the dead descendants of Adam, and the Theotokos who brought forth the living in Christ. The Church derives her motherhood from such elements. This section is mainly concerned with the relationship between the Theotokos and the Church. We have discussed how the Church is identified as the bride of Christ but interestingly some liturgical texts identify the Theotokos with the bride of Christ despite being His mother. For example, the litany of the eleventh hour of the *Agpeya* (Coptic Book of Hours) directs this passage to the Theotokos, "Overthrow the conspiracies of the enemies, shut fast the gates of Hades lest they devour my soul, O blameless bride of the true Bridegroom." This identification helps us understand the presence of an indissoluble union between the motherliness of the Mother of God and the motherliness of the Church.

When Eve sinned, she was a virgin by whom death entered into the world. When Mary obeyed, she was a virgin by whom salvation came into the world. Eve brought forth the descendants of Adam the first whereas Mary gave birth to Adam the second. Likewise, the Church is a virgin mother who gives birth to all who are in Adam the second by redeeming them from being in Adam the first through baptism, that is death and resurrection with Christ. In this manner, we are born unto the Father as members of Christ and Christ is made manifest in those who are born of the Church, the second Eve and the mystical Mary.

At the foot of the Cross, the beloved disciple, John according to Tradition, and the Theotokos stood witnessing the death of God in the flesh. From the cross, Christ committed John to the care of Mary and Mary to the protection of John. We may understand this in a spiritual manner realizing that John being a disciple of Christ put under the care of Mary is a symbol of all of us being disciples of Christ under the care of the Church. We also have a duty to love and protect the Church bringing it to our home just as John brought Mary to his home until the day of her passing away. Just as Mary's body was taken to heaven in glory after her departure, likewise the Church, without dying as Christ promised that the gates of Hades would not prevail against it, will be taken up in glory on the day of the second coming. On this day, Christ will come with the saints in heaven to join them to the saints on earth that the mystical union between the living and the dead may become ever complete.

Pneumatological Ecclesiology

Sadly, many theologians speak of the Church as the body of Christ and bride of Christ and forget about the ever-essential reality of the Church as the indwelling of the Spirit. The presence of the Spirit in the Church is what protects the "traditioning" of dogmas from being compromised. The Spirit is the Spirit of truth and therefore wherever He is, there the truth will be. As Irenaeus of Lyons expresses in his work *Against the Heresies*, "for where the Church is, there is the Spirit of God; and where the Spirit of God is, there is the Church, and every kind of grace; but the Spirit is truth."[20] The following passage describes the role of the Spirit in the prayer of the third hour of the *Agpeya* (Coptic Book of Hours),

> "O Heavenly King, the Comforter, the Spirit of truth, who is present in all places, and fills all, the treasury of good things, and the Life-Giver. Come and dwell in us and purify us from all defilement, O Good One, and save our souls."

When we cooperate with His presence inviting Him to dwell in us, the truth of the gospel is opened before our eyes that we may receive Life, blessings, cleansing, and salvation. It must be noted that life here is not the mere biological life but is *zoë*, the life of the resurrection we receive from Christ. As Christ said, "the Spirit will take from what is mine and give unto you" (John 16:14). Therefore, the Spirit takes the

---

[20] Irenaeus of Lyons, *Against the Heresies*, 3.24.

life and resurrection of Christ and dispenses it to the believers in the sacramental life of the church.

The Spirit is not only the guardian of truth and the life of the Church but is also the One by whom the unity of the Church is protected. This is revealed to us when we read the Old Testament event of the tower of Babel juxtaposed with that of the descent of the Spirit on the disciples in the New Testament. In the rebellion of Babel, people decided to build a high tower with a city to prevent God from destroying them with a flood once more. Sin was the cause of God's intervention of confusing their languages and tongues. In the New Testament, the disciples gathered with one heart praying for the descent of the Spirit. The Spirit came upon them as tongues of fire and enabled them to speak in various languages and tongues. The presence of the Spirit brought them to a place of understanding and unison. Where the Spirit of God is, even the multiplicity of tongues becomes a method of uniting those whose tongues have been multiplied. As Cyril of Alexandria expresses in his *Glaphyra on Genesis*,

> "Thus, in the case of preventing the building of the tower and the scattering of all nations, the multiplicity of tongues was a preconcerted message indicating that at the coming of Christ, this will be the tool of unity by the grace of the Spirit..."[21]

---

[21] Cyril of Alexandria, *Glaphyra on Genesis, II* in Gregory K. Hillis, *Glaphyra on the Penteteuch*. Vol. 137. *Fathers of the Church* (Washington D.C.: The Catholic University of America Press, 2018).

The following quote by the same Cyril in his *Commentary on the Gospel of John* summarizes the work of the Spirit toward accomplishing Church unity,

> "[Christ] wishes indeed the disciples to be kept in unity of mind and purpose, being blended, as it were, with one another in soul and spirit and the bond of peace and brotherly love; and to be linked together in an unbroken chain of affection, so that their unity may be so far perfected [that it] may resemble the natural unity which exists between the Father and the Son... For as we read in the Acts of the Apostles, 'the multitude of them that believed were of one heart and soul,' in the unity that is of the Spirit."[22]

That All May be One

"We were also trying to march towards the recovery of that unity: a goal that still seems so essential to the credibility of the Christian faith in the world at large. How fortunate I feel now—and how grateful I am to God—that He kindled in us... the spirit of this new era, with its renewed sense oof openness and committed fellowship... [E]cumenical openness is not meant to nullify our critical abilities. The encounter itself is only the beginning of a greater process of discernment and distinction... The temptation is great to reduce the ecumenical encounter to mere sentimentality, on

---

[22] Cyril of Alexandria, *Commentary on the Gospel of John*, 2.9, in Joel C. Elowsky (ed.), David R. Maxwell (trans.), *Ancient Christian Texts: Cyril of Alexandria's Commentary on John*, Vol. 2, (Downers Grove: InterVarsity Press, 2015).

the one hand, or zealotry on the other... Indeed, an easy ecumenism may be no ecumenism at all... 'Ecumenism,' as I understand it, refers to a spirit, a way of looking at Christian life, where we recognize that all Christians are bound in brotherhood through the unique figure of Christ and the unique nature of His Gospel. It is a common effort to grow in our understanding of the Truth, to act under the imperative of love, and to share our gifts in the service of those whose lives are improved through such sharing. Ultimately, this becomes a self-enriching way of praising God and partaking in His kingdom."[23]

–Catholicos Karekin I of Armenia

+++

The catholicity of the Church dictates that she longs for the unity of all. The Church being inseparable from Christ ought to work toward the unity of all believers which He sought in His priestly prayer recorded in the Gospel of John. Protecting Church unity was a challenge that Christians had to face from the birth of Christianity. Paul had to admonish the Corinthians to uphold unity because of the various schisms they were falling into. Paul insisted that those who are in the Church ought to believe in one Lord, one faith, one baptism, and participate in one Eucharist. Ignatius of Antioch insisted that the oneness of the eucharist is safeguarded by the one bishop around whom the presbyters, deacons, and congregation are gathered. The validity of

---

[23] Iris Papazian, *Karekin I in His Own Words*, (Vagharshapat: Kerakin I Theological and Armenological Studies Series, 2002), 182, 188, 192.

some bishops' office was challenged by the increase of sectarian and heretical groups that declared their leader a bishop. In response, Irenaeus of Lyons taught that a bishop with a valid priesthood is one who can trace his ordination all the way back to the apostles.

The presence of heretics, schismatics, and apostates dictated that the Church mettles with the question: How do we receive those who have fallen outside the Church back into the Church? Different fathers had different answers to this question prior to the Council of Constantinople. For example, some thought that one who was baptized by heretics or schismatics ought to be baptized once again in the One Church such as Cyprian of Carthage and Augustine of Hippo. Others like Dionysius of Rome and his namesake Dionysius of Alexandria believed that there was no need for rebaptism. When a schism occurred due to terminological difference between Nicene Orthodox followers of Athanasius and other Christians who believed in the faith of Nicaea though without accepting the nuance of *homoousios*, Athanasius received them into communion without any reservation believing that unity of faith trumps unity of terminology. Basil the Great suggested that a rebaptism of those who have been baptized in the name of the Trinity is unnecessary though they must be received through chrismation. After the Council of Constantinople, the Church eventually chose to follow the middle path forged by Basil the Great.

The Council of Ephesus caused a temporary schism between the Churches of Alexandria and Antioch over

Christological terminology. Cyril of Alexandria was able to agree to a statement of reunion that satisfied him and John, the Patriarch of Antioch, which compelled the latter to accept the decrees of the Council of Ephesus. Although the schism lasted for three years and children were born, baptized, and received chrismation during those three years, Cyril readily received them into the Church without requiring re-administration of the sacraments of baptism or chrismation. The unity of faith was enough for Cyril to accept the Antiochian brethren who were only separated in terms of terminology but are united in the substance of their confession of faith. The Council of Chalcedon marked the long-lasting schism between the Oriental Orthodox on the one hand and the Byzantine Orthodox and Roman Catholics on the other hand. In the subsequent decades, Oriental Orthodox saints made the process of returning to communion as easy as possible. Timothy II of Alexandria insisted that Chalcedonians are to be received into communion assuming they confess the Trinity, the incarnation, and the consubstantiality of Christ's humanity with ours. Timothy II did not expect the lay believer to explain whether they believe in one or two natures and did not think that a lay member of the Church should concern themselves with such philosophical and complicated matters. A sterner measure was placed upon clergy who had to write their confession of the Orthodox faith while renouncing Chalcedon.[24] They were able to receive communion immediately upon drafting their confession of faith although they were not able to celebrate liturgical sacraments as clergy except after a year of penance. Timothy insisted on the reception of clergy without reordination encouraging his followers in Alexandria to receive returning clergy ordained by a Chalcedonian patriarch or bishop as if they are ordained by his own hands.

Severus of Antioch, walking in the footsteps of Cyril of Alexandria, engaged in multiple debates with Chalcedonians especially during the reign of Justinian. The efforts of Severus almost reunited the Church if it were not for the Chalcedonian fundamentalism that was growing within the Roman Church. With regard to reception of Chalcedonians into the Church, Severus followed the guidelines of Timothy II and promoted them through the letters he sent to bishops and clergymen who requested his guidance in ecclesial matters.

In medieval times, there were many attempts at reunion between the Byzantines and Armenians who adhered to the Oriental Orthodox Christology of Cyril of Alexandria. Although these attempts mostly failed, they created an atmosphere in which Nerses IV of Armenia (1102-1173 CE) could say, "If one nature is said for the indissoluble and indivisible union and not for the confusion, and two natures for being unconfused and immutable and not for the division,

---

[24] R. Y. Ebied and L. R. A. Wickham, "A Collection of Unpublished Syriac Letters of Timothy Aelurus," *Journal of Theological Studies;* London 21 (January 1, 1970): 365.

both are within the bounds of Orthodoxy."[25] The doctrinal developments in the west eventually compelled the Copts and Syrians because of their geographical proximity to Byzantium and Rome to draw a distinction between their sacramental treatment toward the Eastern or Byzantine Chalcedonians vis. a. vis. Roman Catholics. Coptic medieval canons insist that a Byzantine Chalcedonian is to be received through a confession of faith whereas it is not clear if any canons referring to Roman Catholic reception into Oriental Orthodoxy exist at all. Syriac Christians have often interacted with Assyrian Christians and Chalcedonian Christians in Syria, Iraq, Lebanon, and Jerusalem. These interactions seem to have been mostly positive to the extent that Bar Hebraeus (1226-1286 CE) says in his book *The Dove*,

> "When I had reached the age of twenty, the then living patriarch compelled me to receive the dignity of a bishop. Then it was inevitable for me to engage myself in disquisitions and disputations with the heads of other confessions, interior and exterior. And when I had given my thoughts and meditations to this business during some time, I became convinced, that these quarrels of Christians among themselves are not a matter of facts but of words and denominations. For all of them confess Christ, our Lord, to be wholly God and wholly man, without mixture, nivellation or mutation of natures.

---

[25] James F. Keenan SJ and Joseph Kotva, eds., *Practice What You Preach: Virtues, Ethics, and Power in the Lives of Pastoral Ministers and Their Congregations* (Lanham: Rowman & Littlefield Publishers, 1999), 258.

> This bilateral likeness is called by some nature, by others person, by others hypostasis. So I saw all Christian peoples, notwithstanding these differences, possessing one unvarying equality. And I wholly eradicated the root of hatred from the depth of my heart and I absolutely forsook disputation with anyone concerning confession."[26]

Amidst an Islamically dominated world, no real effort was dedicated toward Christian unity in Egypt and Syria. However, Christian fraternity can be seen in scattered incidents throughout the Middle Ages and toward late medieval times. For example, Cyril IV of Alexandria enjoyed close ties with the Armenian bishop and Greek Patriarch in Alexandria to the extent that the Greek Patriarch entrusted Cyril IV with his flock when he had to be absent. Cyril IV however had an unfriendly attitude toward the Syriac presence in Egypt despite Copts and Syrians being in communion. The boundaries and ties between the various Eastern Christian groups seem to be rather blurry in this era.

The rise of the ecumenical movement in the early 1900s paved the way for various Christian groups to interact with one another in a spirit of love and empathy that provides an atmosphere where each Church can define its boundaries and ties. The Ecumenical movement has aided the Chalcedonian and non-Chalcedonian families to enjoy a better dialogue untainted with the gloomy historical events and bitter memories of persecution. Among the major Oriental

---

[26] Gregory Bar Habraeus, *The Book of the Dove*, trans. A. J. Wensinck (Lieden: Brill, 1919), 60–61.

Orthodox figures that have participated in the Eastern-Oriental dialogue have been Metropolitan Paulos Gregorios and Fr. V. C. Samuel from the Malankara Church, HH Mor Ignatius Zakka Iwas I from the Syriac Church, HH Pope Kyrillos VI, HH Pope Shenouda III, HE Metropolitan Bishoy of Damietta, Fr. Tadros Malaty, and Deacon. Dr. Joseph (Athanasius) Faltas from the Coptic Church. The unofficial and official agreed statements between the Oriental and Eastern families of Orthodoxy illuminate the Chalcedonian controversy with the clarification that the controversy is mostly terminological and political rather than theological or substantial. Although no sacramental eucharistic union has been reestablished between the two families, pastoral statements have been established between select Churches from both families to facilitate sacramental collaboration on the lay level such as the agreed statement between the Greek and Coptic Patriarchates of Alexandria with regard to inter-Orthodox marriages and the statement between Antiochian and Syriac Patriarchates of Antioch with regard to intercommunion on the lay level in cases of inter-Orthodox marriage or absence of clergy from one patriarchate.

On the Western front, the Oriental Orthodox communion enjoys a dialogue with a number of Churches such as the Roman Catholic Church, the Anglican Church, and the Lutheran Church. Although these dialogues have not come to fruition to the extent the Oriental-Eastern dialogue has, they have provided an ethos of philanthropic collaboration between various Christian groups that have been separated by theological differences and historical circumstances.

The Oriental Orthodox Church, having inherited the legacy of Severus of Antioch, finds it necessary to believe her communion to possess the fullness of truth and Orthodoxy though without condemning other denominations as graceless. Amidst the Chalcedonian Controversy, Severus boldly proclaimed to the zealots of his age that though a schism exists, he cannot say for sure that this negates the possibility of the sacramental presence and grace in the Chalcedonian camp. As such, Severus was committed to the cause of ecclesial unity and engaged in possible ways to restore union between the Chalcedonian and non-Chalcedonian parties. The Oriental Orthodox Church walks in the same footsteps hoping to restore Church unity, upholding the truth of her faith, and refraining from judging the sacramental status of other Apostolic Christian communities.

Chapter 6

The Sacramental Life of the Church

What is a Sacrament?

A sacrament or a *mysterion* can be defined as the main task of the Church in which Christ dispenses Himself to the congregation that they may *together* come to experience He who is not only beyond knowing but also beyond unknowing. This definition is a combination of Augustine's thoughts on the Church as Christ dispensed through the sacramental life of the Church and Gregory of Nyssa's thoughts on us being in communion with God through His activities though in His essence, He is beyond anything we can conceive. For many centuries, the Orthodox Church lived without giving a set number of sacraments. All that happens within or by the agency of the Church was considered sacramental. Thus, it is no surprise that some manuscripts would count the tonsuring of monks or the funeral prayers as sacraments. Later, when the Church had to deal with Catholic and Protestant missionaries, it became essential to canonize the sacraments to a set number and as such the Church declared seven sacraments of the Church in which the work of the Spirit is manifest through the liturgical rituals. These seven sacraments are baptism, chrismation, repentance and confession, eucharist, priesthood, matrimony, and unction of the sick. Oftentimes we read the following definition for a sacrament, "a sacrament is an outward sign of an invisible grace." This definition was coined by Augustine and further formulated by Thomas Aquinas. With time, it has become more associated with the scholastic theology of the Roman Catholic Church. The definition may be understood in an Orthodox manner if it is understood that the grace given in the sacraments is an element of the presence of Christ and the Spirit themselves in each and every sacrament. This provides the mystical element of the sacrament which scholasticism might tend to avoid or dismiss.

Saved through Water and Fire

Before creation, the Spirit of the Lord hovered over the face of the waters before the creation of the cosmos. During baptism, the Spirit hovers over the face of the waters in the baptismal font that we may be created anew in Christ. Noah was saved through the arc from the flood of water. Christians are saved through baptismal water from drowning in the flood of materialism and selfishness. When Eliezer, Abraham's servant, had to find Isaac a wife, he asked God for the one who would draw water from the well. Likewise, Christians by passing through the water of baptism, they become worthy of partaking in the marriage of Christ and the Church as new members of the Church. Jacob struggled with God before He was renamed Israel and came to cross the river so he can return home. Likewise, catechumens struggle with God through learning the faith before they can cross the river of baptismal waters and return to the home of the Father. Moses and Joshua crossed the Red Sea and the

Jordan River with God's presence in the staff and the Ark of the Covenant. Likewise, Christians pass through baptismal waters with Christ's presence as He was Himself baptized in the Jordan. Elijah proved that the God of Israel is the true God by pouring water upon the sacrifice that was to be consumed by the divine fire. Similarly, Christians are baptized in water before they receive the gift of the fiery Spirit in Chrismation. Elisha cleansed Naaman the Syrian through water just as Christians are cleansed from sin through water and Spirit. In the life of Christ, He was baptized in the Jordan, an event which none of the Evangelists omit. Christ met the Samaritan woman at a well where He identified Himself with the Living water whom no one can draw from and thirst again. Christ healed the man born blind by sending him to wash in the pool of Siloam signifying how baptism creates spiritual eyes for us by which we can see God.

Water was often seen in a negative light in ancient mythology as a symbol of chaos and disarray. When Christ entered the waters of baptism, He cleansed the water and subdued it. When He walked on water, He manifested the power of His divinity over the waters. Now we go through water in order to partake of His power and life. While we say in the creed that baptism is received for the remission of sins, one cannot limit the benefits of baptism to forgiveness of sins. As John Chrysostom says,

> "You see how many are the benefits of baptism, and some think its heavenly grace consists only in the remission of sins, but we have enumerated ten

honors it bestows! For this reason, we baptize even infants, though they are not defiled by personal sins, so that there may be given to them holiness, righteousness, adoption, inheritance, brotherhood with Christ, and that they may be Christ's members."[27]

Basil the Great summarizes the effects of baptism in the following homily on baptism,

> "Baptism: This is what buys back captives, forgives debts, and indelibly marks its recipients. It is a heavenly chariot, the sure promise of the kingdom, the grace of adoption."[28]

Therefore, we baptize infants not for the remission of sins per se but because of the added blessings that come with it. Oriental Orthodox Churches possesses the same belief in the efficacy and centrality of baptism yet expresses this through two major methods. The Copts, Syrians, Ethiopians, Indians, and Eritreans perform baptism by full immersion under water whereas the Armenians occasionally adopt the practice of sprinkling with water.

Following baptism, believers receive the Holy Spirit to ever dwell in them never leaving them. In the early Church, the apostles laid their hands on the heads of the believers and in this manner, the newly baptized believer would receive the Spirit. With the expansion of the Church, it became

---

[27] John Chrysostom, *Baptismal Catechesis* in Scot McKnight, *It Takes a Church to Baptize: What the Bible Says About Infant Baptism*, (Ada: Brazos Press, 2018), 17.

[28] Basil the Great, *Exhortation to Baptism*.

necessary to find another method of receiving the Spirit. As such, the Church began practicing the anointing with oil done by a bishop or any of the presbyters representing him that the believer may receive the gift and seal of the Holy Spirit. The Oriental Orthodox Church performs chrismation immediately after baptism in imitation of Christ whom upon coming out of the water had the Spirit descend upon Him in the form of a dove.

Church fathers commented on this incident shedding light on Christ being the One who sends the Spirit as God and receives the Spirit as man being both God and man simultaneously. In the Gospel of John, John the Forerunner attests that the Spirit came upon Christ and remained upon Him. This teaches us that when the Spirit dwells in man, He never departs unless the person blasphemes the Spirit i.e., apostatizes. The Spirit being sent by Christ comes upon those who are baptized in order to make them "christs" i.e., anointed ones who have received the chrism and anointing of the Holy Spirit. In being anointed, we are reminded of our place as kings and queens in the kingdom of God as in old times kings were the ones who were anointed to become the Lord's christs. We are chrismated to derive our identity as kings and queens in the kingdom of God from Him who is the Heavenly King of Kings. Similarly, we receive the general priesthood of believers which entails that we become stewards of our own selves working our own salvation, stewards of the Church serving in loyalty and love, and stewards of the world exercising care for and authority over the whole of creation.

We receive the grace of baptism and chrismation

"from Jesus Christ, who is the faithful witness, and the first begotten of the dead, and the prince of the kings of the earth. Unto him that loved us, and washed us from our sins in his own blood, and has made us kings and priests unto God and his Father."

Revelation 1:5-6

We are reminded of the words of the Coptic Orthodox Liturgy of Basil the Great, "[Christ] granted us the birth from on high through water and Spirit. He made us unto Himself a congregation and sanctified us through [the Father's] Holy Spirit." Having become baptized believers invested with the Holy Spirit, we are made ready to receive the medicine of immortality, the Eucharist.

The Eucharist

The Divine Liturgy is the summit of all that is sacramental in the Church. It consummates our membership in the Church as we partake of the mystical body of Christ. Metropolitan Ishaq, bishop of Christian education in the Syriac Orthodox Church, introduces the liturgy by introducing the incarnation as the act upon which the Liturgy is founded. Ishaq sees the incarnation as the way Christ "became like us, that we may become like Him. He became man willingly that He may make us sons of God and partakers of the Holy Spirit."[29] Ishaq elaborates on the

---

[29] Ishaq Sakka, *Commentary on the Liturgy According to the Rite of the Antiochian Syriac Orthodox Church*, (Atchaneh: The Syriac Orthodox Convent of Mor Jacob Baradaeus Publications, 2003), 26.

incarnation as the project of our deification contrasting our perception of deification with that of God, he writes,

> "The project of deification man has planned (you will become like God) was a failing project. As for the project [of deification] planned by Jesus Christ, it was a successful project."[30]

Later, Ishaq regards the unity of men as an outcome of our union with Christ accomplished through the Eucharist. Ishaq quotes the order of Pentecost of the Syriac Church which reads, "O Christ, our God, unite us through our mingling with You."[31] To Ishaq, the ultimate objective of Christianity is union with God accomplished through the Eucharist. Ishaq sums up the Eucharist as he says, "when we become 'the body of Christ,' we all become united with one another forming the mystical body of Christ, one body not many bodies."[32]

In the Liturgy, we commemorate the coming of Christ, His life, His death, His resurrection, and His ascension into heaven as our First fruit. This commemoration is not seen as a mere memorial but rather as a re-living of salvific events that transcend the limitations of time and space. Every time, we eat the body and drink the blood of Christ, we live in the sacrifice of Christ which was done once and for all. Though this sacrifice took place in the past, it derives its infinite outcomes from the infinite identity of the One who sacrificed

---

[30] Sakka, 26.
[31] Sakka, 49.
[32] Sakka, 51.

Himself. As such, we participate in the Cross as an event that *is* taking place not as an attempt to remember what once *was*.

In the Old Testament, the tabernacle was the meeting place of God and man. Only Moses and the High Priest could indeed meet God there. For the rest of the year, the Arc of the Covenant was hidden from the eyes of all in the Holy of Holies. When Christ was crucified, the veil covering the place where the Holy of Holies would have been was torn in two that there may be no barrier anymore between God and man.[33] When Christ was crucified, He became the meeting place in whom God and man can be united once more. In His outstretched arms, the tribes of the earth are invited to come together in unity in the Incarnate Word. Through the Cross, God descends in ultimate humility not only to become human but also to become a dead human being who descends into Hades. Simultaneously, we ascent to meet with God in the cross as ones who are identified with the crucified Christ. This meeting is only accomplished in the Liturgy where we receive the body of Christ from the Golgotha of the Orthodox altar. The Liturgy is the place where we offer Christ in the Eucharist for the life of the world and offer the world in thanksgiving to Christ. In baking the bread that is to become the body of Christ, we take the most basic form of food and offer it as representation of all food. In mixing the wine that is to become the blood of Christ, we take the most basic drinks of wine and water and offer them as a

---

[33] When Christ was crucified, there was nothing in the Holy of Holies as the Arc of the Covenant was lost. However, the Holy of Holies in the new temple continued to be seen as the holiest place of the temple where God dwells.

representation of all drink. Together, bread and wine are offered as the body and blood of Christ who is offered for the life of the world.

In the Liturgy: Christ offers Himself as an acceptable sacrifice; we offer bread and wine in thanksgiving; we offer the body and blood of Christ that we may receive the grace of immortality and deification; we offer the world redeemed in Christ to God the Father; we offer the pain and joy of the world to God that He may give us grace through the body and blood of Christ; Christ offers us in His body and blood to the Father. Christ is offered and we are offered. Christ is the offeror and we are offerors with Him. We no longer do anything apart from Him. Rather, we are in Him and He is in us by virtue of being members of His body who have partaken of His flesh and blood.

Having covered the mystical element of the Eucharist, it is necessary to turn our attention to the ritualistic element of the Liturgy. The Liturgy is seen by Orthodox Christians in a twofold manner: Liturgy of the Word and Liturgy of the Eucharist. This organization of liturgical elements finds its roots in the apparition of Christ to the two disciples at Emmaus. Christ met the two disciples who did not recognize Him. They continued not to recognize Him even as He showed them from the Scripture (i.e., the Old Testament) that He must suffer and rise. Their confusion persisted even when He would exegete the meaning of the Old Testament (i.e., the New Testament). They only recognize Him when He breaks the Eucharistic bread at the table. When He disappears, He is manifested in the bread which becomes His body. When they eat His body, they become His body, the Church. Similarly, we might hear the Scriptures of the Old Testament and the New Testament and fail to hear or understand who Christ is. This is because at this level we are trying to fit the infinite in our finite minds. However, when we eat the body and blood of Christ, we become united to Him and as such we come to recognize Him. Only then can the ambiguities of Scripture become illuminated before our eyes. Therefore, the Church insisted since its birth in the voice of the Church Fathers that Scripture cannot be interpreted apart from the Church. The Church reads and interprets the Scripture eucharistically, meaning in the light of the crucified and risen Christ as He appears on the altar and begins opening the Scriptures for us.

Our eyes which were opened in Adam and Eve to behold our nakedness and ignorance are now shut. Rather, our spiritual eyes are now opened with the disciples on their way to Emmaus as we behold Christ on the altar interpreting Scripture. In this manner, we hear the Word of God in the Liturgy of the Word and eat the Word of God in the Liturgy of the Eucharist. Though Armenian, Coptic, Tawahedo, and Syriac rites differ in order and style, their theological understanding of the place of the Liturgy in the life of the Church is one and the same. The beauty of the Liturgy as the meeting place of God and man, heaven and earth, is best summarized in the words of Dionysius the Aeropagite as he says,

> "I think we must now go inside the sacred things and reveal the meaning of the first of the images.

We must look attentively upon the beauty which gives it so divine a form and we must turn a reverent glance to the double movement of the hierarch when he goes first from the divine altar to the far edges of the sacred place spreading the fragrance and then returns to the altar. For the blessed divinity, which transcends all being, while proceeding gradually outward because of goodness to commune with those who partake of him, never actually departs from his essential stability and immobility. Enlightening anyone conforming as much as possible to God, the Deity nevertheless maintains utterly and unshakably its inherent identity. Similarly, the divine sacrament of the synaxis remains what it is, unique, simple, and indivisible and yet, out of love for humanity, it is pluralized in a sacred variegation of symbols. It extends itself so as to include all the hierarchical imagery. Then it draws all these varied symbols together into a unity, returns to its own inherent oneness, and confers unity on all those sacredly uplifted to it."[34]

The Liturgy here is not to be lived in isolation from the heavenly and eternal liturgy that is to come. We begin the Liturgy here as Orthodox Christians from the various tribes of the earth that we may live the divine presence here before we behold it beyond this world in the light of God with the cloud of saints. We partake of the heavenly banquet here on earth in the Liturgy and go to the world thereafter to begin

---

[34] Pseudo-Dionysius the Areopagite, *Pseudo-Dionysius: The Complete Works.*, trans. Colum Luibheid (Mahwah: Paulist Press, 1987), 212-213.

the Liturgy of the world where we invite members of the world to become members of the Church. When Christ comes again, we will begin the Liturgy of the heavenly banquet that will never end.

Royal Priesthood

> *"A priest is always one who stands before God on behalf of others, interceding for them, offering their sacrifices. Jesus Christ is the one and only High Priest, the archetype of all priesthood. He did not offer the sacrifice of himself for his own sake, but for the sake of the world, to reconcile the world to God."*[35]
>
> –Metropolitan Paulos Mar Gregorios

+++

Christ having offered Himself once and for all as the ultimate sacrifice for the life of the world and the salvation of humankind, He has declared Himself as the High Priest. Christ is the priest par excellence. Those whom we call priests are participants in the one priesthood of Christ. When a man is selected to become a member of the diaconate, priesthood or bishopric, he officiates sacraments not on account of a priesthood intrinsic to him but rather as one who derives his functionality from his participation in the priesthood of Christ. Each rank of the clergy has its sacramental and administrative functions that developed over the centuries of Christianity. The role of the bishop

---

[35] Paulos Gregorios, *The Meaning and Nature of "Diakonia,"* (Kottayam: Mar Gregorios Foundation, 2015), 48.

came to be an extension of that of the apostles. Thus, bishops are called successors of the apostles. The bishop's role is to be an intercessor for his congregation praying for them, educating them and preserving them in the Orthodox faith. The presbyters should mainly be concerned with the education of the congregation and the performance of the sacraments of the Church. The role of deacons entails the more social services of the congregation such as serving tables and outreaching the poor and widowed. Certainly, these roles used to overlap in the past. We hear John the Evangelist and Apostle call himself a presbyter in the opening of his second letter in the New Testament. It was common for deacons to perform sacraments such as baptism. Now, deacons would perform a baptism only in extreme situations with the priests performing the sacrament being the norm. With the decline of the role of deacons in the churches of Syria and Alexandria, the administrative and social roles of deacons have been taken over by presbyters who now serve the sacraments, teach the congregation, outreach the poor and widowed, and occasionally even serve tables.

The priesthood the bishops and presbyters derive from Christ is inseparable from the fatherhood they derive from God the Father. A bishop or a presbyter who is not a father is compromising the foundation of his role. The servitude of Christ as the suffering Servant for His people is mimicked by the deacons. A deacon who is not sacrificing himself for the congregation is no *diakonos*, literally servant.

Let us conclude with the words of the Ethiopian Anaphora of Athanasius which outlines some of the roles of the priests and deacons:

> "O priests, you are the bright eyes of God; look to one another, investigate your people prudently in order that no adulterer, murderer, idolater, thief or liar should stand and join you in prayer... Rebuke the sinner as him who is your brother, and scold him openly if he hath committed a sin unto death. Advise the wicked to leave that way and submit himself unto God so that he may forgive him. O deacons, lights and messengers of the church, drive away from it the wolf, so that it may not be among the sheep; the kite, that it may not be among the doves, and take away the tares so that they may not be (found) among the wheat. You investigate that which is without and not that which is within; but that which is within God knows and examines with his light."[36]

Reconciled with God

"Why art thou impatient to be off when He has not given to thee? Stay long and knock at the Physician, and beseech Him, and bring the tears of repentance and besprinkle His doorstep; entreat much; and if for love He give not to thee, yet to importunity He

---

[36] Marcos Daoud, *The Liturgy of the Ethiopian Church* (Great Britain: Kegan Paul, 2005), 139.

will not be able to deny all her requests. Be insistent at the Physician's door, and give not over; for if thou be backward He will not bind thee up. Why standest thou still? Importunity knows how to obtain mercy of Him; and unless He give to her she will not suffer Him to depart."[37]

–Jacob of Serug

+ + +

There are a few terms that need to be defined before we delve into the meaning of the sacrament of repentance and confession such as sin, repentance, and forgiveness. Sin is defined by many as wrongdoing or choosing an evil course of action. This definition does not reflect the biblical or patristic tradition. James writes, "Therefore, to him who knows to do good and does not do it, to him it is sin" (James 4:17). Sin is not about the wrong you commit but rather the good you choose not to do. In our patristic heritage, we are taught that sin has no concrete existence or being. Just as darkness is lack of light, sin is lack of being, life, and good. In religion, the main categories are good and evil. One is to do good and avoid evil. In Christianity, the main categories are life and death. The Didache insists that these are the two ways we are to choose from. Whenever we do not choose life, we are sinning toward ourselves and are distancing ourselves from life and drawing nearer to death. Gregory of

---

[37] A Homily of Mar Jacob of Serûgh, "On the Reception of the Holy Mysteries," translated by R.H. Connolly, *The Downside Review 27* (1908), 651.

Nyssa teaches that our spirituality is either experienced as an ascent or descent. We cannot simply remain stationary.

Repentance is the English translation of the Greek word *metanoia*. The prefix *meta* refers to change while *noia* or *nous* refers to the mind. Repentance as such is the change of mind from death to life from sin and collaboration with the devil to a union with God. Our understanding of the word forgiveness impacts our understanding of God to a large extent. Many assume that sin is about offending God and that when we repent, we compel God to forgive us. This could not be further from the truth. God acts upon man but man does not act upon God. When God became man and was crucified for us, He offered us forgiveness once and for all. When we repent, we, by the grace of God, approach the mercy and forgiveness which are readily available in the Cross of Christ. The following story can help us understand this complex concept:

A man lived in the desert and there was only one river from which he could draw water. He decided to walk away from the river until he could no longer find the river. He was thirsty and had no way of quenching his thirst. Thus, he asked God to guide him once more to the river. God heard his prayer and the man changed his direction and went back once more to the river and drew water.

The man is a type of you and me. His thirst is a type of sin. The river is a type of forgiveness. His prayers are a type of our plead for God's mercy and compassion to be with us as we find the river of forgiveness. The change of direction is a type of repentance by which we find forgiveness. Notice how in this parable, you cannot be forgiven apart from God, yet you are not acting upon God. God is sovereign and mighty. He is not acted upon by us. Rather, as a compassionate Father, God offered His forgiveness once and for all through the Cross of Christ and He guides us through the Spirit whenever we desire to return to draw near Him and His forgiveness.

What I have indicated here thus far is the personal element of repentance. Now let us proceed to the other dimensions of repentance in the Orthodox Church. Repentance is perfected when it is performed in Church through the sacrament of confession. Confession involves the presence of a presbyter or bishop whose work is twofold: a spiritual guide for the Christian and a representative of the Church. The role of the spiritual guide is to offer the person the spiritual medicine needed for the spiritual sickness a person is suffering from. As the believer reveals their weaknesses, the father of confession offers his helping hands in prayer for the believer and in advising them as they grow in their spiritual quest for union with God. In revealing our weaknesses, we break our ego that desires praise and accuse our ego of our sins instead. This causes our ego to shrink and allows us to have a real being in Christ where we decrease, and He increases. Only those who break their ego in the admission of their sins are made worthy, by God's grace, for the partaking of the broken body of Christ.

A father of confession is not merely an advice bank but is a physician of souls who is able to diagnose sickness and ailment, offers spiritual medicine and journeys along the person. Another role of the presbyter in the sacrament of confession is to represent the Church. If we truly believe that we are members of the body of Christ, we must believe that every sin we commit on our own impacts the body of Christ as a whole. Hear what Paul says about those who sin while they are members of the body of Christ, "Do you not know that your bodies are members of Christ? Shall I then take the members of Christ and make *them* members of a harlot? Certainly not" (1 Corinthians 6:15). Thus, when we repent, we need the witness of the Church that we are back as fully functional members living a life worthy of the calling by which we were called. We are reconciled to the Church through the blood of Christ shed for the remission of sins. The presbyter offers his witness through the recitation of the absolution or prayers of forgiveness while we are granted spiritual healing from the past sin and the preventative medicine of prayer, fasting, vigil, and watchfulness to avoid the temptations that are to come. In this manner, the Church protects her children from spiritual sickness preserving them in her holiness.

Healing of Us All: Anointing of the Sick

In the previous chapter, we explored the sacrament of repentance and confession as a sacrament of spiritual healing. This chapter deals with the sacrament of holistic healing, the anointing of the sick. Though this sacrament is prayed when someone is physically sick, the presbyter prays for their ailments of body, soul, and spirit. In the litany of the Gospel in the Coptic Orthodox Church, the presbyter addresses God as "the healing of us all." We are healed by realizing our place in Christ, the physician of bodies and souls. In being anointed, we are reminded of our royal status in Christ as kings and queens in His kingdom even as we suffer. Our condition does not impact our identity in Christ. The words of James shed light on the physical and spiritual dimensions of the rite of anointing the sick,

> "Is anyone among you sick? Let him call for the elders of the church, and let them pray over him, anointing him with oil in the name of the Lord. And the prayer of faith will save the sick, and the Lord will raise him up. And if he has committed sins, he will be forgiven."
>
> James 5:14-15

There is no true healing apart from being in a state of repentance. If God's will is for the sick to depart, the Church submits herself to the divine will of God praying for the departed person in the hope of the resurrection, the ultimate healing and hope of the human race.

Hope of Us All: Funerals

The *Sh'himo* (Syriac Book of Hours) contains a prayer for the departed that goes as follows,

> "Blessed are the dead who have slept and rested in peace; the flesh of the Son is buried with them as a pledge; he will cast down the walls of Sheol for them with violence and they will hear his voice and will go forth to meet him with speed."

The body of Christ is buried in our bodies through our partaking of the Eucharist. When we are buried, His body is buried with us that we may arise with Him unto eternal life. The Orthodox Church prays funerals not simply for the comfort of the family and friends of the departed but rather to help us realize that our death is death with Christ and therefore we live on the hope of the resurrection of the dead. Many have provided theories and speculations as to what happens to the soul after death, heaven, hell, paradise, and hades. Reality is that what we know about the details of the coming age and our lives after death is minimal and quite unnecessary for our salvation. What matters most is the undisputed reality and historicity of the Resurrection of the Son of God in whom our resurrection will come to fulfillment. We believe that Christ is risen and that we have no resurrection apart from him. We believe in a judgement day in which Christ will appear to judge the living and the dead. Christ Himself declared that this judgement will not be a court like system. Rather, it is a spiritual judgement in which the words Christ has "spoken will judge [us] in the last day" (John 12:48). How would such judgement take place? We ought to confess our ignorance in humility. The time we would spend on speculating ought to be spent on living a repentant life preparing for the age to come.

The Oriental Orthodox Church like all apostolic Churches prays for the souls of the departed. There are many reasons for this which we can find in the writings of the fathers of our Church. I will be listing here only a sample of these sayings,

> "The believers are permitted to pray for those who have apostatized and died before repenting if their apostasy is the result of their bitter sufferings. It is permitted for the believers to support the relatives of those apostates in their sorrows and prayers. For fervent prayers are powerful and efficacious to perform miracles and through these prayers, they become worthy of the mediation of our beloved Redeemer and He grants them the forgiveness of their sins."[38]

> "Not in vain did the Apostles order that remembrance should be made of the dead in the dreadful Mysteries. They know that great gain results to them, great benefit."[39]

> "We believe that the souls for which petitions are offered, there will be great benefits for them when we offer the ever fearful and holy sacrifice."[40]

In a nutshell, we pray for the dead out of the hope of the resurrection which is implanted in our hearts since the day we were baptized, died, and resurrected anew with Christ. Whether our prayers change the destiny of the dead or not is irrelevant. We still ought to follow the fathers of the Church who taught that memorials, petitions, and giving of alms are to be given for the souls of those who have passed away. This is due to the fact we belong to the same body of Christ and as such we are to pray for them as they pray for us. Our prayers for the dead are a testimony of our sense of

---

[38] Peter, 17th Pope of Alexandria, in Iris Al-Masry, *Story of the Coptic Church* (Alexandria: St. George Sporting) 2003, 131.

[39] John Chrysostom, *On Philippians*, Homily 3 (on Philippians 1:24).

[40] Cyril of Jerusalem, *Catechetical Lectures*, 23.9.

belonging to the same church whether we are among the living on earth or those who have departed the world and live in Christ. In praying for the dead, we are reminded to pray for ourselves to complete our days in the world in love and fear of God knowing that we will be united to the departed when our time in this world comes to an end.

The Sacrament of Love

> *"A deacon holds the crowns while the celebrant recites a prayer over them: 'O Lord, Who did adorn the sky with luminaries: the sun, the moon and all the stars; O God, Who did crown the earth with fruits, flowers and blossoms of all kinds; O Jesus Christ Who did crown kings, priests, and prophets... O God, Who encircled the ocean like a crown around all the earth... put Your right hand upon the heads upon which these crowns are placed.'*
>
> *Then, the celebrant, waving his right hand over the crowns, blesses them crying aloud: "Blessed and perfect be these crowns and the heads upon which they are placed."*
>
> *–The Rite of Matrimony in the Syriac Orthodox Church*

+ + +

The sacrament of matrimony is the sacrament of unity of Christ with His Church. Almost all Orthodox Churches read passages of Scripture in their rite of matrimony that remind us that marriage is holy because of it being an extension of the marriage of Christ and the Church. As Paul puts it,

> "Husbands, love your wives, just as Christ also loved the church and gave Himself for her, that He

might sanctify and cleanse her with the washing of water by the word, that He might present her to Himself a glorious church, not having spot or wrinkle or any such thing, but that she should be holy and without blemish. So, husbands ought to love their own wives as their own bodies; he who loves his wife loves himself. For no one ever hated his own flesh, but nourishes and cherishes it, just as the Lord does the church. For we are members of His body, of His flesh and of His bones. 'For this reason, a man shall leave his father and mother and be joined to his wife, and the two shall become one flesh.' This is a great mystery, but I speak concerning Christ and the church."

Ephesians 5:25-32

In this passage, we are reminded that when Adam saw Eve, Adam said that "a man shall leave his father and mother and be joined to his wife" (Gen. 2:24); and these words are to be applied to Christ and the Church. We are also reminded that each marriage is an extension of the ultimate marriage of Christ and the Church. Interestingly, there are three walks in the same chapter that Paul addresses before he delves into marriage: the walk in love (Ephes. 5:2), the walk as children of light (Ephes. 5:8), and the walk of wisdom (Ephes. 5:15). Only when one is able to set his eyes on these walks can they be ready to participate in a marriage through which they can be saved. As a quote often attributed to John Chrysostom expresses, "If a man and a woman marry in order to be companions on the journey from earth to heaven, then their union will bring great joy to themselves and to others."

Traditional marriage in the world as we know it is a union of love between a man and a woman. Christian marriage involves God as the head of the union of love being a giver and a recipient of love in the triune relationship of love between Himself, man, and woman. Marriage in the world involves an exchange of rings as a sign of the covenant between man and woman. The marriage of Christians involves the exchange of rings as well but is accompanied by the service of crowning by which the couple is reminded of the royalty of the Christian marriage as it is a union of a king and a queen in the kingdom of God. They are also reminded of the element of martyrdom in marriage symbolized by the crowns. Martyrs being witnesses of Christ through the shedding of their blood remind married couples that they are called to become martyrs as well through breaking their ego daily in submission to one another in love, respect, and honor. The typology of Christ and the Church on the one hand, and the man and woman on the other hand, is mentioned throughout Orthodox services. Consequently, men are always reminded of their role as priests in their household. Likewise, women are reminded to collaborate with their husbands in sober obedience aiming to bring salvation to their household. The salvation of every household falls predominantly on the shoulders of the man who is to transform his home into a Church, yet such task cannot be truly accomplished apart from the wife's willful participation. Therefore, even though Christian marriage resembles the traditional marriage of the world in many aspects, it is blessed with being taken into the kingdom of God to become a royal and priestly marriage by which the couple are granted the potential to emulate the martyrs and become united with God.

Consecrate a Fast

> *"This is the sign of Christianity. However, much man should do and how many justifying works he should perform, he should feel that he has accomplished nothing. And when he fasts, he should say, 'I have not fasted.' When he prays, let him think, 'I have not prayed.' Persevering in prayer he should say, 'I have not persevered. I have only begun to practice asceticism and to labor.'"[41]*
>
> –Macarius the Great, Homily 26

+ + +

Anyone with any knowledge of the Orthodox Church is aware that it includes numerous periods of fasting. This is an attempt to call the believers to live the commandment our ancestors failed to fulfill in Eden. If Adam and Eve, being immature, failed to fast from the fruit of the tree, then we, who are in Christ, ought to abstain from food in order to keep the body under control. Certainly, other religions put an emphasis on the fast for the purpose of self-control. Christian fasting derives its uniqueness from the theology ascribed to it by the Orthodox Church. In the numerous fasts, the Orthodox spend the morning in abstinence from any food or drink to emulate the angels whose food and drink is the

---

[41] George A. Maloney, *Pseudo-Macarius: The Fifty Spiritual Homilies and the Great Letter* (Mahwah: Paulist Press, 1992), 167–68.

spiritual praise of God. When breaking their fasts, the Orthodox are on a vegetarian diet to remember the prelapsarian state of Adam where he ate from the fruits of the earth without shedding the blood of any animal. Due to the weakness of man, the Coptic and Syriac Orthodox Churches prescribed fasting seasons where consumption of fish and seafood is permitted. The Armenian Apostolic Church permits her members to consume dairy products and eggs throughout select periods of fasting. The Syriac Orthodox Church of Antioch has recently shortened many of the ecclesial fasts. Even more, the Syriac Orthodox Church began celebrating the feast of the Nativity on the Western calendar for the sake of her members who mostly reside in the West and find it difficult to keep the feast if it is on the old calendar and falls on a working day.

The fasts of the Church are not intended to be a form of bodily abuse. Rather, it is an attempt to live the Kingdom of God before we reside permanently in it after the second coming. As Fr. Matthew the Poor puts it in one of his sermons, "fasting is an attempt to live without food." It is an attempt to take crumps of time and transform them into moments of eternity through a life of fasting and prayer. The fasts prescribed bridge space and time inasmuch as they help us participate and relive the memories of the life of Christ and the Church: the nativity fast is a preparation for the coming of Christ; the Great Lent is a commemoration of Christ's encounter with men and women during His ministry and a preparation for His life giving sufferings; the fast of Holy Week is a time of co-suffering with Christ in vigorous asceticism remembering His lifegiving passions and preparing for His Holy Resurrection; the fast of the Apostles is a reminder of the ascetical life of the early Church; the fast of the Theotokos reminds us of the ascetic life she led until she was made worthy to receive Christ in her womb; the fast of Jonah is a local six day fast which the Syriac Orthodox Church inherited from the Chaldeans in the Church of the East. The fast is now observed by both Copts and Syrians for three days only falling a few weeks before the Great Lent reminding the congregation that Jonah was a type of Christ with whom we are about to fast forty days and forty nights.

Although fasting is an essential part of the life of the Church, we cannot reduce fasting to a mere observance preordained by the Church. Fasting can be observed in a more personal manner. Those who are preparing for the reception of illumination in baptism are to observe a fast under the guidance of their spiritual guide. Some choose to fast on their own especially monastics to train their bodies to need less food. Others fast before receiving the sacrament of matrimony asking God to preserve their marriage in purity.

Fasting as such is no longer about self-control alone as it is in the rest of world religions. Rather, it is a way of co-living and co-suffering with Christ. Despite the greatness of fasting, there are fasts which are not acceptable before God. Pope Shenouda III in his book *Spirituality of Fasting* lists six fasts that were not acceptable before God: (1) the fast performed for the praise of men, (2) the fast of the Pharisees i.e., a prideful fast, (3) a fast with an erroneous goal i.e., the fast of the mob that decided not to eat or drink until they kill

Paul, (4) the fast of a sinful congregation such as those who lived at the time of Jeremiah, (5) the fast bereft of mercy and almsgiving, and (6) the fasts that are not for the sake of God such as those who fast for medical reasons.[42] Through fasting, we become truly able to control the belly and the passions that cause our descent and with Christ we ascent to become more Godlike inasmuch as that is humanly possible.

---

[42] Pope Shenouda III, *The Spirituality of Fasting* (Cairo: Dar El Tebaa El Kawmia, 1990).

Chapter 7

Christian Anthropology

Who is Man?

"The human is a rational creature of God, having come into being according to the image of his Creator. According to the image of God the human came into being."

--Basil the Great, On the Origin of Humanity, XI

+ + +

There are, however, major distinctions between God as the archetype and the human being as the image. For example, God is wholly invisible. Man, however, is both visible and invisible. As such, we have a double identity. We share visibility with the rest of the created order while we share invisibility with God. Basil elaborates,

> "I recognize two human beings, one the sense-perceptible, and one hidden under the sense-perceptible, invisible, the inner human. Therefore, we have an inner human being, and we are somehow double, and it is truly said that we are that which is within. For I am what concerns the inner human being, the outer things are not me but mine... Therefore, the body is an instrument of the human being, an

instrument of the soul, and the human being is principally the soul in itself."[43]

Therefore, humanity is to be the mediator between God and the rest of creation. The soul is of extreme importance as the prime mover of the human being. The body is the instrument by which the soul affects this mediation between God and man. This compelled numerous Christian theologians to call the human being, the priest of the world. To be the priest of the world is to offer the world an understanding of God through our merciful heart toward creation. As Isaac the Syrian says, "a pure heart is a heart merciful toward all created beings."[44] Likewise, humans are to offer the world to God through their constant thanksgiving for the created order that they are to use and enjoy.

Such sublime calling suggests that humanity ought to exercise rulership over the world by serving it and being served by it in a mutual loving relationship. Due to the fall (which we will examine later), humanity ceased to accomplish its intended role and began rather to abuse the world having it serve its ill desires. Basil comments on this tragedy,

> "First the power to rule was conferred on you. O human, you are a ruling being. And why do you serve the passions as a slave? Why do you throw away your own dignity and become a slave of sin?

---

[43] Basil the Great, *On the Human Condition,* trans. Nonna Verna Harrison, (Crestwood: SVS Press, 2005), 36.

[44] Metropolitan Hilarion Alfeyev, *The Spiritual World of Isaac the Syrian* (Kalamazoo: Cistercian Publications, 2000).

For what reason do you make yourself a prisoner of the devil? You were appointed ruler of creation, and you have renounced the nobility of your own nature."[45]

Humans are either masters or slaves. As masters, we are to serve the world and offer it to God in thanksgiving. As slaves, we have the world serve the passions of our flesh which become our masters. We must come to balance the relationship between our body and soul. We must come to serve the world and be served by it as loving masters of the world and as servants of God simultaneously.

The Greek word referring to the human being is *anthropos*, which literally means "one who looks upward." While humans are distinct from other living and mobile creatures in many ways, their ability to look upwards stands out. Gregory of Nyssa comments on the posture of humans in the following way,

> "But man's form is upright, and extends aloft towards heaven, and looks upwards: and these are marks of sovereignty which show his royal dignity. For the fact that man alone among existing things is such as this, while all others bow their bodies downwards, clearly points to the difference of dignity between those which stoop beneath his sway and that power which rises above them."[46]

Gregory is mainly concerned with the royalty of humanity in relation to other living creatures. It is important

---

[45] Basil the Great, *On the Human Condition*, 37.
[46] Gregory of Nyssa, *Creation of Man*, 8.1.

that we note that every royalty in humanity is bestowed from above. James writes, "Every good and perfect gift is from above, coming down from the Father of the heavenly lights, who does not change" (James 1:17). God, known in Judeo-Christian literature as the King of Kings, offers humanity sparks of His own kingship.

For humanity to continuously resemble God, we ought to constantly fix our eyes on God. We ought to become wise for wisdom "is a reflection of the eternal light, a spotless mirror of the working of God, an image of his goodness" (Wisdom 7:26). Every image is a mirror that reflects an archetype. We are mirrors and the more we direct ourselves toward God, the more we resemble Him and reflect Him to all other beings. Regarding this, Gregory of Nyssa writes,

> "For he who has truly come to be in the image of God and who has in no way turned aside from the divine character bears in himself its distinguishing marks and shows in all things his conformity to the archetype."[47]

When the fall takes place, humanity ceases to look toward God and focuses instead on materialism and egoism. Consequently, man ceases to resemble God.

Ancestral Sin

When Adam and Eve sinned by the consumption of the forbidden fruit, they were banished from the paradise of joy.

---

[47] Gregory of Nyssa, *The Life of Moses*, trans. Abraham J. Malherbe and Everett Ferguson (Mahwah: Paulist Press, 1978), 136.

Many of us have questions about the nature of the tree of knowledge. Others have questions regarding the nature of the punishment our ancestors received. I believe Gregory the Theologian answers these questions clearly in his *38th Oration*,

> "This [human] being He placed in Paradise, whatever the Paradise may have been, having honored him with the gift of Free Will (in order that God might belong to him as the result of his choice, no less than to Him who had implanted the seeds of it), to till the immortal plants, by which is meant perhaps the Divine Conceptions, both the simpler and the more perfect; naked in his simplicity and inartificial life, and without any covering or screen; for it was fitting that he who was from the beginning should be such. Also, He gave him a Law, as a material for his Free Will to act upon. This Law was a Commandment as to what plants he might partake of, and which one he might not touch. This latter was the Tree of Knowledge; not, however, because it was evil from the beginning when planted; nor was it forbidden because God grudged it to us… But it would have been good if partaken of at the proper time, for the tree was, according to my theory, Contemplation, upon which it is only safe for those who have reached maturity of habit to enter; but which is not good for those who are still somewhat simple and greedy in their habit [i.e., life]; just as solid food is not good for those who are yet tender, and have need of milk. But when through the Devil's malice and the woman's caprice, to which she succumbed as the more tender, and which she brought to bear upon

the man, as she was the more apt to persuade, alas for my weakness, he forgot the Commandment which had been given to him; [Adam] yielded to the baleful fruit; and for his sin he was banished, at once from the Tree of Life, and from Paradise, and from God; and put on the coats of skins... that is, perhaps, the coarser flesh, both mortal and contradictory. This was the first thing that he learned—his own shame; and he hid himself from God. Yet here too he makes a gain, namely death, and the cutting off of sin, in order that evil may not be immortal. Thus his punishment is changed into a mercy; for it is in mercy, I am persuaded, that God inflicts punishment."[48]

The sin of Adam and Eve is not mere eating of a forbidden fruit but rather attempting to enter a state they were not prepared for. Not only was it trespassing a state they are not ready for, but it was also even done for the wrong motivations i.e. becoming like God, apart from God, at the advice of the serpent. The punishment inflicted upon them is seen by Gregory the Theologian as a form of mercy by which God put a limitation on evil. This parallels the Coptic Orthodox Liturgy attributed to Gregory the Theologian which says, "You, O my Master, have turned for me the punishment into salvation." The Church believes that God, even when He is inflicting the due justice, is doing this out of mercy. In a way, all punishments stem from divine mercy and as such are considered redemptive punishments rather than retributive punishments. As Basil the Great says,

---

[48] Gregory of Nazianzus, *Oration 38*, XII.

"Neither is God's mercy without judgment, nor is His judgment without mercy."[49]

Returning to the question of ancestral sin, we should examine the consequences of the sin of Adam and Eve and how the outcome of their sin became part of our lives. First, we must understand how the fathers interpreted the word sin. Sin is called *amartia* in Greek, meaning "to miss the mark." The fathers of the Eastern Church interpreted sin as nonbeing and lacking in substance, the way darkness is the absence of light. We see this interpretation of sin in the writings of Athanasius of Alexandria in his book *On the Incarnation*. Less than a century later, the Pelagian controversy began. Pelagius believed that the sin of Adam had no implications whatsoever on other human beings who came after him. Adam's sin had no ontological impact on him or his descendants in Pelagius' theory. To Pelagius, Adam would die regardless of sinning or not. The punishment of Adam was a mere moral issue according to Pelagianism. In combating this theory, the famous theologian of Western Christianity, Augustine, took the other extreme of claiming that sin has a substance of its own which became mingled with the nature of Adam. Sin as such is inherited from generation to the next through the intercourse of men and women, and in this manner, all children are born with the sin of Adam and Eve as an essential part of their humanity. In Augustine's system,

---

[49] Sister Agnes Clare Way, trans., *Saint Basil Exegetic Homilies* (Washington, D.C: The Catholic University of America Press, 1963), 233, http://archive.org/details/fathersofthechur013929mbp.

Adam who was created immortal is now mingled with sin that he lost his immortality.[50] The exception to this rule in Augustinian thought was of course Jesus Christ as He was sinless as God and having been born without the seed of man, He was also sinless as man. Those who are influenced by Western theology insist on the inheritance of the sin of Adam and Eve as a substance in our flesh. In trying to justify their position, they use verses such as "Therefore, just as through one man sin entered the world, and death through sin, and thus death spread to all men, because all sinned" (Romans 5:12) and "Behold, I was brought forth in iniquity, and in sin my mother conceived me" (Psalm 51:5). In the course of this chapter, it will be shown how neither the Pelagian or Augustinian formulations paralleled the theology of the Eastern fathers such as Athanasius of Alexandria, Cyril of Alexandria, and Severus of Antioch, etc. Various commentaries on the aforementioned verses, that are often used to justify the Augustinian position, will also be shared.

Let us begin with how the fathers interpreted passages such as Romans 5:12 and Psalm 51:5 before delving into the way the fathers explained the concept of ancestral sin and what we inherited. In a homily on Romans, John Chrysostom says,

---

[50] This is to be contrasted with the Eastern notion of Adam being mortal though preserved in immortality through grace rather than immortality being inherent to him. As such, when Adam sins, Eastern fathers see his mortality as a return to the state he was to be in had the grace preserving him in a state of immortality not been there to begin with.

"How, and in what way? He enquires whence death came in, and how it prevailed. How then did death come in and prevail? Through the sin of one. But what means, for that all have sinned? This; he having once fallen, even they that had not eaten of the tree did from him, all of them, become mortal."[51]

Severus of Antioch had to respond to Julian, a heretic who believed that sin was commingled with the body of all men. Julian relied on a false interpretation of Psalm 51 among other passages of scripture. In response, Severus of Antioch writes about Psalm 51:5,

"Paul writes to the Galatians saying that he was set apart from his mother's womb to serve the gospel and preach to the gentiles. Here, he does not mention the middle part of his life in which he was a persecutor of the Church of God and a blasphemer who tried to destroy the Church. In this manner, he has left behind him the shadow as if his entire life was known for its righteousness. Similarly, those who lived a sinful life distant from God after having lived in disobedience to the divine commandments and precepts are considered and called distant from God, Who foreknew their future state from the moment of their birth… David in a similar line of thinking returned to himself and attempted to justify himself by saying, 'I was brought forth in iniquity and in sin my mother conceived me.' It is as if David is saying I have fallen into sins such as adultery and murder

---

[51] John Chrysostom, *On Romans Homily 10* (on Romans 5:12).

without remembering that I lived according to the truth and the Law. I revert all responsibility of my life as if it was in its entirety in sin considering it immersed in iniquity and sin from the moment I was formed and conceived in the womb of my mother."[52]

Romans 5:12 is interpreted in the light of the rest of Scripture suggesting that the sin of Adam caused death to enter into the world that such death belonged to all even though the sin of Adam belonged to him alone. Others have also sinned and incurred death upon themselves, but their sin was distinct from that of Adam. As for Psalm 51, Severus makes it plain that this is a metaphor, or a figure of speech, found throughout scripture and does not have to be taken to prove anything about the notion of ancestral sin which was nonexistent in the Jewish theology David might have been aware of.

Athanasius of Alexandria taught that man was mortal inasmuch as he was created out of nothing. Because of divine grace, Adam was protected from mortality because of the external grace which God granted him. When Adam and Eve chose to sin, they were deprived of the grace which once protected them from mortality (*On the Incarnation* 3, 4). As descendants of Adam and Eve, we are born in the same state deprived of the grace which protects us from the sting of mortality and death. You can choose to read more on this in Athanasius's masterpiece *On the Incarnation*. This brief

---

[52] Severus of Antioch, *Contra Additiones Juliani, Corpus Scriptorum Christianorum Orientalium* 29.

explanation shows that the Pelagian extreme of sin having no impact on the descendants of Adam is not acceptable, neither does the Augustinian extreme of the guilt of Adam being in us have a place in Eastern Patristic thought. It is clear in Athanasius's thought that sin is not material, neither does it have a substance of its own, but rather an absence of what is good.

In the East, Cyril of Alexandria addressed the question of ancestral sin multiple times. In his *Glaphyra on Genesis*, he writes,

> "Because the innovator of sin deceived Adam in the beginning, and because of his slumber, he was made guilty. In this manner, Adam was led to death and the sentence of death was cast to extend over all people for the disease has spread to the branches that came out of him… Thus, the Creator tended to his creatures finding a new origin for the human race in the One who ascended to the first [state] of incorruption. Just as Adam the first was made of clay and caused us death having bound us with the nets of corruption, likewise we have been sealed with the stamp of incorruptibility by becoming like Adam the second (Christ) by means of the Spirit."[53]

Thus, we can understand that what we have inherited from Adam was the corruption, death, and certainly the inclination to sin which spread its poison to our nature. This

---

[53] Cyril of Alexandria, *Glaphyra on Genesis*, I in Gregory K. Hillis, *Glaphyra on the Penteteuch*, Vol. 137, *Fathers of the Church* (Washington D.C.: The Catholic University of America Press, 2018), 62-63.

is not to be confused with the actual act of eating of the fruit of the tree. In another instance, Cyril writes,

> "We must examine how the penalty of Adam, the first father, which he deserved due to his disobedience, was transmitted to us... From incorruption, he became corrupt and liable to death. When the fallen man began to beget children in death, meaning those who were born of him, we were born corrupt having been born of a corrupt one. In this manner, we inherit the curse of Adam. However, we were not punished because we were guilty with Adam nor because we disobeyed the sin which he committed. But, as I said, because man became dead, he transmitted the curse to the children he begat, meaning that we became mortal because we are born of one who is mortal... Thus, we can conclude that the universal and general curse of the disobedience of Adam is corruption and death."[54]

It is evident that we have received the curse of the sin; otherwise, we would not be often inclined to sin, be mortal, and corruptible. However, we must understand that what we received is the result of being born in the condition of death and corruption in which Adam and Eve were found. This is not to be confused with sin being transmitted to us as an inheritance or substance. As Cyril recounts, "it is foolish to believe that the efficacy of the curse of the earthly and

---

[54] Cyril of Alexandria, *Against Those Who Imagine that God has a Human Form*, 8.1 in Cyril of Alexandria, *Against Those Who Imagine that God has a Human Form*, George Awad Ibrahim (trans.) (Cairo: GC Center Publishing Press, 2013), 67-68.

human Adam was transmitted to the rest of the human race as an inheritance."[55] Sin and its effects are not transmitted through marriage as an inheritance but rather we are born mortal because we are born from one who is mortal. Therefore, we may conclude that Cyril sees us as ones living in a condition of sin and death resulting from the error of Adam, but not as ones whose nature is mingled with sin.

This continued to be the Church's line of thinking in the years after Athanasius and Cyril as we see Severus responding to Julian of Halicarnassus saying,

> "The sin of those who brought us forth, meaning the sin of Adam and Eve, is not mingled with our natures and essence... We are born mortal having been born of mortal fathers, yet we are not sinful because of our birth from mortal fathers. This is because sin has no substance and is not transmitted through childbearing from parents to their children. If the case was otherwise, no one born of a sinful father can become righteous no matter how great an ascetic he is because the attributes of nature would be unchangeable."[56]

Our birth from a mortal man makes us mortal but sin is a choice that each person is responsible for. Severus once said in a homily, "Sin is spiritual blindness by which the

---

[55] Cyril of Alexandria, *Glaphyra on Genesis*, I in Gregory K. Hillis, *Glaphyra on the Penteteuch*, Vol. 137, *Fathers of the Church* (Washington D.C.: The Catholic University of America Press, 2018), 63.

[56] Severus of Antioch, *Contra Additiones Juliani*, Corpus Scriptorium Christianorum Orientalium 296, Louvain.

sinner punishes himself rather than an inheritance we carry with ourselves."[57]

Copto-Arab fathers of the Coptic Orthodox Church walked in the same footsteps with understanding ancestral sin. For example, Abi Isaac Ibn Abi El-Fadl Ibn El-Assal (13th century) writes,

> "The sin of Adam caused his death and the death of all people. The domination of death over Adam was because of his disobedience of His Lord having eaten from the tree. As for the dominion of death over them, it is caused by the sins they commit. Adam showed the sin that causes death, but the sins committed differ between him and his children... As for the saying that death had dominion over those who did not sin, it refers to the prophets and messengers such as Moses and Peter to whom no significant sin was attributed but rather involuntary minor trespasses and laps."[58]

Likewise, Ibn Katib Qaisar (13th century), in a commentary on Romans, interprets scripture in the same light as John Chrysostom and Cyril of Alexandria when he writes,

> "Sin has entered into the world through the mediation of man, and by it, death had dominion over all from Adam to Moses, not because they

---

[57] Severus of Antioch, *Homily XXI*, Corpus Scriptorium Christianorum Orientalium, Louvain.

[58] Ibn El-Assal, *Ablagh Al-Wasa'el Ila Elm Al-Rasa'el* (Maryout: St. Mina's Monastery Publishing Press), 89.

sinned similarly to Adam in his sin of eating of the tree, but because they committed other sins."[59]

In the modern era, Fr. Manassah Youhanna (19th century) wrote in his book *Life of Adam*:

> "The original sin is not a trespass we have committed by our own will. God does not condemn us to punishment considering it committed by our will. Rather, it is the death of the soul, and such death is the absence of life. The life of the soul dwells in the justifying grace. Thus, original sin is the absence of the initial righteousness or being void of the justifying grace and the loss of the initial free state, because his [i.e., Adam] descendants are born without such grace."[60]

Similarly, Bishop Athanasius of Beni Suef (20th century) writes in his *Commentary on Romans*,

> "Some say that we inherit the sin of Adam and that we accept the faith that this sin may be forgiven. The Scriptures say otherwise through Jeremiah the prophet (Jeremiah 31: 29-30) and Ezekiel the prophet (Ezekiel 18:2-4). Sin has made her dwelling with humans, and we partake of sin and are to give an account for our own sins (James 1:13-14). If we were to give an account for the sin of our father Adam, such sin would have been forgiven since salvation took place and Adam was forgiven (Zechariah 9: 11-12) … No matter how

---

[59] Ibn Katib Qaisar, *Commentary on the Epistle to the Romans* (Cairo: Society of the Children of the Coptic Orthodox Church Press), 108.

[60] Fr. Manassah Youhanna, *Life of Adam*, (Cairo: al-Mahaba Publishing Press), 105.

great the sins of men are, even if gathered altogether, they remain limited. But the salvation Jesus offers is infinite."[61]

All of these fathers agree that Adam sinned and that we sin, but the sins committed differ. All sins lead to death and corruption. Death and corruption have become part of the condition in which we live. This does not however mean that sin is transmitted to us through sexual intercourse or as an inheritance. This would be opposed to the justice of God and would be contrary to the bed of marriage being undefiled. Scriptures would not call the bed undefiled if it were the mode of transmitting sin from generation to generation. Admittedly, some saints such as Augustine would speak in terms of "inheriting sin." However, every attempt should be made to read this in an Orthodox manner not in the sense of sin being a substance to be inherited, neither should it be taken in the light of marriage being the mode of sin transmission.

Many pages and quotes have been dedicated to this topic, even though it is not a fundamental dogma of the Church like the Trinity, the Incarnation, etc. This is because misunderstanding ancestral sin can easily affect our understanding of ourselves as human beings, God, and our spirituality. If we understand ourselves as helpless creatures infused with sin against our will since the day we are born, then we will not have the motivation to work out our salvation. Even the wound of our inclination to sin, which

---

[61] Athanasius [Bishop of Beni Suef], *Commentary on Romans* (Beni Suef: Metropolis of Beni Suef Publishing Press), 1997, 65

was caused by the sin of Adam, is undone by baptism in which we put on Christ and are born to the newness of life living through grace and faith rather than in fear of Satan and death. In understanding the economy of salvation, ancestral sin would play a role in how we see God. There is a major difference between a god who punishes me for a sin I did not do versus the God who turns the punishment into salvation as per the words of the Gregorian Liturgy of the Coptic Church. God is not a tyrannical being punishing humans for what they do not do but rather is a loving being who comes to lift humans up from the pit of their fall and releases them from their inclination to sin and death by uniting Himself with them through His Only Begotten. Though we now understand that we do not inherit sin, we must be aware that Adam and Eve desired becoming gods apart from God and that this is no different from what we often do. Many times, we desire carnal knowledge, pride, and ego and put these above our desire for God. In doing this, we are no different from Adam and Eve. This compelled the fathers to compose liturgical texts such as the opening of the Coptic Liturgy of Gregory the Theologian in which the presbyter says, "I ate of my own free will. I laid aside Your law by my own counsel. I neglected Your commandments. I brought upon myself the sentence of death." We might have not sinned with Adam and Eve because we were not living but we ought to be watchful lest we fall in the same sin by our own free will.

Cosmology

This section explores what the Oriental Orthodox Church believes regarding the relationship between God, creation, and man. Though many Church fathers speak about this threefold relationship, I will mostly rely on the writings of two contemporary theologians of the Oriental Orthodox Church, namely Bishop Poemen of Malawi, Egypt, and Metropolitan Paulos Mor Gregorios of Delhi, India.

God and Man

There is an intimate relationship between the incarnation of God and the divinization of man. In fact, the acts of the incarnate Christ are reflected on the glory and divinization of humanity. As Gregorios puts it,

> "When Christ, as the divine-human person, raises up the dead, heals the sick and the paralyzed… Christ glorifies God and God glorifies humanity in Christ."[62]

Through the Incarnation,

> "[t]he glory of humanity becomes revealed when human beings do the works of God. In these works [of the incarnate Word], God and humanity are simultaneously glorified."[63]

---

[62] K. M. George, *Paulos Mar Gregorios: A Reader*, (Philadelphia: Fortress Press, 2017), 281.

[63] George, *Paulos Mar Gregorios*, 281.

Human performance of divine works has two major constraints: human freedom and human limitedness. Gregorios insists that

> "[h]uman freedom is too important for Eastern spirituality to be made subordinate to any kind of law, whether of Church or state. People are meant to be kings, not obedient servants. They are not slaves in the house of God."[64]

Despite such freedom man enjoys, man is bound by his measure as a created being limited by time and space. Though man performs divine acts, man does not go beyond "the 'measure' of the nature of humanity, for so to go out would be to cease to exist." Furthermore, man is limited as an earthly being whose "full potential is not at all evident here." These limitations, however, do not obstruct the journey of man toward divinization as "the very nature of humanity is to be like God, for that is what it means to be created in the image of God. The more humanity becomes like God, the more it becomes itself. Divinization is humanization."[65] The ultimate success of human divinization is accomplished when man becomes "the visible presence of God himself" not as the "master of the universe in his own right, but only as the image of the invisible God," who is able "to heal humanity as well as the civilization."[66]

---

[64] George, *Paulos Mar Gregorios*, 142.

[65] Paulos Mar Gregorios, *Cosmic Man: The Divine Presence: The Theology of St. Gregory of Nyssa (ca. 330 to 395 A.D.)*, (New York: Paragon House, 1998), 230.

[66] George, *Paulos Mar Gregorios*, 240.

God and Creation

Gregorios places creation in the world as a midpoint between God as true being and non-being. The universe stands between these two poles, as this

> "which has been brought from non-being into existence by the true Being, and which continues in existence, both depending on the true Being and participating in the energies of the true Being."[67]

Therefore, the fundamental distinction between God and creation is that God is "good-in-itself, being-in-itself" while the world is "good-by-participation, being-by participation on the other."[68] The world depends on God for its subsistence while God is self-subsistent. Though this discontinuity between God and creation exists, there is a sense of unity seen vividly in the act of the incarnation. In the incarnation, God becomes matter as the Son assumes His human nature formed of the elements of the earth. This body carrying the elements of the earth

> "was transfigured on Mount Tabor, crucified on the tree and came out through the mouth of the tomb, the body in which he appeared to the disciples, in which he ascended to heaven. Matter and nature participate in the redemption."[69]

---

[67] Paulos Mar Gregorios, *Cosmic Man*, 108–9.
[68] Paulos Mar Gregorios, *Cosmic Man*, 116.
[69] Paulos Mar Gregorios, *Cosmic Man*, 140.

In this manner, creation, within Christ's body, has ascended into heavens and sat at the right hand of God. Therefore, there is an intimate relationship between Creation and Creator in Christ. Beyond the ascension of Christ, healing and transforming the cosmos becomes the task of man co-working with the divine energies. In the Incarnation, the unity of God and man is offered by Christ, the God-man, to man. Similarly, beyond the ascension, unity of God and creation is offered by man, the divinized-creation, to creation.

Man and Creation

There is a continuity between man and creation as,

> "the same creative energia of God which has brought matter into existence, and through that same creative impulse brought into being successive stages of existence—the vegetable kingdom, the animal kingdom and the human realm."[70]

Though the common source is the energies of God, there remains a major distinction between creation and man as the latter

> "is not an object for the cosmic forces to mold at their will. He is free. This means that he is not a passive subject, acted upon by the universe, but is

---

[70] Paulos Mar Gregorios, *Cosmic Man*, 223.

capable of understanding and acting upon the universe."⁷¹

Not only is man active and free but he is

> "the image of God. The meaning of his being is not to be... derived primarily from the fact that human nature recapitulates in itself all lower forms of life as well as inorganic matter."⁷²

Therefore, man, who is both the image of God and the being in whose nature all lower forms of life are recapitulated, is able to act upon the world reclaiming its harmony with God. Methods of acting upon the world are summarized in three steps by Gregorios in the following manner,

> "(a) dealing with it to create the good through understanding and manipulation, but without idolizing it or being totally absorbed by it; (b) caring for it as one care for the body, or as a priest cares for his people, and developing it; and (c) dealing with it through symbol and ritual to transcend it and to relate oneself to the mystery of the Creator whose energy constitutes it... Only a combination of the three can make us fully human."⁷³

Therefore, man acting upon creation makes man fully human, an allusion to his deification as Gregorios understands divinization as humanization. Furthermore, it

---

[71] Paulos Mar Gregorios, *Cosmic Man*, 273.

[72] Paulos Mar Gregorios, *Cosmic Man*, 273.

[73] George, *Paulos Mar Gregorios,* 274.

enhances the state of the world as man continues to redirect the cosmos toward a genuine experience of God through His sustaining and creative energies. In this manner, *Cosmic Man becomes the Divine Presence in Creation*. According to Gregorios, this presence takes place through,

- (a) the transformation of persons by separation from evil and cleaving to the good;
- (b) the transformation of society itself…
- (c) the transfiguration that goes on through the work of the Spirit in Person… the outcome of which will manifest itself only on That Day.[74]

The work of Gregorios outlines deification in the light of anthropology, cosmology, and the harmony between God, man, and creation. His writings articulate the gap between the current state of the cosmos and the potential the cosmos has upon man journeying toward deification taking his intended position within the cosmos as the vessel of divine presence.

Time and Eternity

The opening words of Genesis, "In the Beginning," suggest that an element of time is present within creation. Creation comes to exist in time i.e., there was a time when creation was not. On the fourth day, God says, "Let there be lights in the firmament of the heavens to divide the day from the night; and let them be for signs and seasons, and for days

---

[74] Paulos Mar Gregorios, *Cosmic Man*, 223.

and years" (Genesis 1:14). Time is created before man was created and the duty of man is to "redeem the time" (Ephesians 5:16). Many have a negative view of time for various reasons such as: lack of control over time, a reminder that one cannot change the past, or a reminder that we are aging and are headed toward mortality, etc. Orthodox Christianity does not turn a blind eye to the problem of time but rather heals our perception of it. Our worship is rooted in a calendar that commemorates feasts of the Lord and feasts of the various saints throughout the year cycle. While different churches within Oriental Orthodoxy might use different calendars, the Church is committed to celebrating the same feasts though the time of celebrating them may differ.

The Liturgy is the healing place of time par excellence as it is the place in which time and eternity intersect. A logical understanding of the liturgy as a living memory is that it is concerned with things of the past. A spiritual understanding of the liturgy as a living memory makes the previous explanation furthest from the truth. The liturgy is a commemoration of the birth, life, ministry, passion, resurrection, and ascension of Christ which are historical events that took place in the past. Simultaneously, it is a commemoration of the second coming which shall come to pass in the future. In the Church, we boldly declare that we remember the past which has already taken place and the future which is to come. This suggests that the Church is able to redeem the time taking us beyond the boundaries of temporality toward a vision of eternity where the past, present, and future are laid before us on the altar in Christ who is above time. As such, the Church is rooted in time through its calendar and in eternity through its ability to remember the past and future in the present through the liturgy and the eucharist. This is the fruit of the incarnation in which the eternal God bends the reality of temporality through the taking of human flesh endowed with a rational soul in time. As Christians, we are called to have time and eternity intersect through converting historical and chronological moments of time into eternity by infusing the time of our life with prayers that aid us in experiencing eternity in time. We are called to transform every moment of time into the acceptable time or year of the Lord; the Lord who surpasses time and is beyond eternity. In a nutshell, the incarnation causes eternity and time to intersect and the continuation of this intersection is the work of the Church through her sacramental life in general and Eucharistic life in particular.[75]

Salvation

> *"They likened the high priest, to our Savior, the true Sacrifice, for the forgiveness of sins. He who offered Himself, as an acceptable sacrifice, upon the Cross, for the salvation of our race. His good Father, smelled Him, in evening, on Golgotha, He opened the gate, of Paradise, and restored Adam, to his authority. Through Mary, the daughter of*

---

[75] Bishop Poemen, *An Orthodox Vision of the World*, (Cairo: al-Mahaba Publishing Press).

> *Joachim, we learned of the true Sacrifice, for the forgiveness of sins."*
>
> – *Coptic Theotokion of the Sunday Midnight Praises*

+++

Church Fathers commented in various ways on the salvation offered to humanity by God through the incarnation. There are a variety of models and analogies they used to describe the "so great a salvation" offered to us (Heb. 2:3). This chapter aims to shed light on how different models are to be understood in the light of the Orthodox faith. Prior to delving into soteriology, it is necessary that we affirm that no analogy or model portrays the fullness of the salvific work the Father has done for us by the Son through the Spirit. A few elements of our faith regarding God, salvation, and ourselves must be acknowledged before we examine the various models the Fathers produced in their literature. First, God is unchangeable and as such the salvation offered for us cannot cause a change in the changeless God. Furthermore, God acts out of His own will as the Sovereign Being unlike human beings who often act out of necessity. Second, salvation ought to cause an impact and a change within us as ones who were once distant from God and now come to experience Him. Third, the salvation offered for us must involve all three persons of the Trinity and must also emphasize the whole life of Christ. Analogies that satisfy all three criteria I just shared with regard to God, man, and salvation are closest to the fullness of truth while others need more nuance and light for them to fit the aforementioned Orthodox conventions.

When God created man in His image and after His likeness, man was to aim toward attaining the likeness of God in communion with Him. When Adam sinned, humanity sought similitude to God apart from God causing an imbalance in the cosmological plan God intended for the world and for man as the priest and king of the world. Instead of communicating the divine presence to the rest of creation, humanity allied itself with the devil having been inclined toward sin and distorting the image which God inscribed in man. Therefore, a change has occurred in humanity causing it to be in need of a recreation, a renewal, or a regeneration.

Pre-Nicene Fathers spoke of salvation in moral terms where the Incarnation takes place primarily for the sake of teaching humans how to emulate the Son, who is the image they were originally created in. For example, Clement of Alexandria, a second century theologian venerated in the Coptic and Syriac Churches, taught that Christ was primarily a Teacher showing humanity how to live a moral life. Clement dedicated his book *The Pedagogus* to this theme of Christ as Teacher. Irenaeus of Lyons relied on Paul who often juxtaposes Adam the first, in whom we sin, and Adam the second, in whom we have a new heavenly life. Irenaeus then presents Christ as One who comes into the world of history and recapitulates the events of history in Himself. Christ's saving work is to revisit the various events in which Adam sinned, reverses the event, and then renews it. Irenaeus uses multiple examples to illustrate his point of which I will only share two: First, Adam and Eve sinned in the garden because of their pride, gluttonous desire for the fruit, their beholding of the fruit and finding it pleasant to the eye, and a carnal desire for the wisdom that comes with eating. Christ revisits, reverses, and renews the previous events by humbly accepting to be tempted by Satan in the desert, rejecting the gluttonous temptation of turning the stone into bread, rejecting the pleasure of the eyes that beheld all the kingdoms of the world, and rejecting the carnal desire for power to fall from the pinnacle of the temple unharmed. Second, Adam and Eve sinned in a garden by eating the fruit of a tree at the advice of Satan, a fallen angel. Christ is born of a Virgin who submits to the angel of God, is handed to be executed in a garden, and is crucified on a tree. Irenaeus lists many other parallels between Adam and Christ to teach us that what Adam ruins for his descendants, Christ fixes for those who are in Him.

Paul uses various themes to present the work of God in creation through Christ such as the model of atonement, payment of debt, and the victorious Christ. Unfortunately, the first two models Paul taught have been misinterpreted in medieval times by Anselm of Canterbury whose work became widespread among various Christian theologians in the East and West today. I will not delve into how his theory does not parallel the Orthodox vision of salvation as it is beyond the scope of this book. I hope to share with you, however, the Orthodox interpretation of these Pauline models through the lens of Post-Nicene Church Fathers. Words like justice, wrath, debt, ransom, sin, penalty, and punishment are words we would hear often in the model of atonement. Each of these terms: (1) is found in Scripture, (2) has an Orthodox interpretation, and (3) can be misinterpreted due to our preconceived notions about the use of the term or because of unorthodox influence. Let us begin setting our definitions from the writings of the Church Fathers.

Justice

Our perception of justice tends to be informed by our context in which justice is a legal form of being fair through using a system of reward and punishment. To our modern ears, the carrying out of justice entails rendering the appropriate punishment for a misdeed. Scripture tends to have a different idea of justice. In the Old Testament, the justice of the law demanded that a woman who is found to have committed adultery was to suffer execution. One would imagine that a just man would be one who executes the law in this scenario. However, when Joseph finds that Mary is with a child before he knew her, he chose to put her away secretly. But note how Matthew the evangelist records this event, "Then Joseph her husband, being a just man, and not wanting to make her a public example, was minded to put her away secretly" (Matthew 1:19). Justice as such was not in the execution of the law but in the mercy shown to Mary whom Joseph falsely accused of adultery prior to the apparition of the angel to him. This should not come as a surprise as Greek uses the word *dikaiosynee* to simultaneously indicate justice and righteousness. Our inclination to set justice and righteousness or mercy as polar opposites is a result of the fall and as such this dichotomy does not exist in God.

This might explain why John Chrysostom would say the following words regarding divine justice,

> "What can come up to this excess [of goodness]? He not only did not demand justice, but even gave His son that we might be reconciled. They that received Him were not reconciled, but even slew Him. Again, He sent other ambassadors to beseech, and though these are sent, it is Himself that entreats. And what does He ask of us? 'Be ye reconciled unto God.' And he did not say, 'Reconcile God to yourselves;' for it is not He that bears [has] enmity, but you; for God is never at enmity with us."[76]

Despite our sin, God does not see us as enemies. Our sin cannot inflict a change on God because He is changeless and thus His perception of us as His beloved creatures does not change. Thus, the Father reconciled the world to Himself in Christ whom He sent (Corinthians 5:19). Although this sounds more merciful than just from our human perspective, God does not render His acts of mercy toward creation as a contradiction or a compromise of His justice. Simply put, there is no dichotomy in God, and this includes justice and mercy or righteousness and love. Indeed, our sense of justice itself would be scandalized by the cross as it is the execution of the righteous for the unjust while our justice would entail that we would receive the judgement of death ourselves as the offenders.

---

[76] John Chrysostom, *Homily 11* (on 2 Corinthians 5:11-21).

Wrath

Divine wrath or anger are another difficult concept that we ought to understand in a divine way rather than imposing our fallen human experience on God. Many saints, including Cyril of Alexandria and John Chrysostom, insist that when Scripture uses "wrath" in relation to God that this is a form of anthropomorphism, meaning that human attributions are being used to describe God who is naturally indescribable. Using the word "wrath" is the closest analogy our limited brain can comprehend to realize that sin produces a state of being distant from God. Anthony the Great in the *Philokalia* describes divine wrath in the following words,

> "God is good, dispassionate and immutable. Now someone who thinks it reasonable and true to affirm that God does not change, may well ask how, in that case, it is possible to speak of God as rejoicing over those who are good and showing mercy to those who honor Him, while turning away from the wicked and being angry with sinners. To this it must be answered that God neither rejoices nor grows angry, for to rejoice and to be offended are passions; nor is He won over by the gifts of those who honor Him, for that would mean He is swayed by pleasure. It is not right to imagine that God feels pleasure or displeasure in a human way. He is good, and He only bestows blessings and never does harm, remaining always the same. We men, on the other hand, if we remain good through resembling God, are united to Him; but if we become evil through not resembling God, we are separated from Him. By living in holiness, we

cleave to God; but by becoming wicked we make Him our enemy. It is not that He grows angry with us in an arbitrary way, but it is our own sins that prevent God from shining within us, and expose us to the demons who punish us. And if through prayer and acts of compassion we gain release from our sins, this does not mean that we have won God over and made Him change, but that through our actions and our turning to God we have cured our wickedness and so once more have enjoyment of God's goodness. Thus, to say that God turns away from the wicked is like saying that the sun hides itself from the blind."[77]

Therefore, we can conclude from this passage that God does not get angry with us but rather we, by becoming wicked, make Him our enemy. God's unchangeability is not only applicable in the case of anger but also in the case of honor and dignity. It became the custom of many western theologians to rely on the Reformed notion of God the Father being angry due to sin bringing Him dishonor.[78] This cannot be further from the truth. God is above human reach and as such our sin cannot inflict a change on His honor or dignity. Moreover, the scripture says that "God so loved the world

---

[77] G.E.H. Palmer, Philip Sherrard, and Kallistos Ware (eds.), *The Philokalia: The Complete Text Vol. I*, (London: Faber & Faber, 1979), 150.

[78] Anselm began the vision of sin dishonoring God which was later exaggerated by reformers who combined this idea with divine wrath and total depravity of human beings. Their way of bridging this judicial gap between the righteousness of God and depravity of humanity was the theory of penal substitutionary atonement where God pours out His wrath on Jesus on the cross for humanity to avoid the punishment they were due because of their sin.

that He gave up His Son" (John 3:16), rather than God so hated the world and was angered because of human sin that He sent His Son to take His anger out on Him. The Fathers see creation and salvation as intertwined to the extent that they call salvation a recreation. Therefore, we can deduce that if God created the world out of His love, pleasure, and goodwill rather than necessity, then He must have saved the world out of the same love, pleasure, and goodwill. The rules of necessity and changeability which control human beings have no place in God.

Debt/Ransom

Given the materialist and consumerist world we live in, we are conditioned to think of debts as payments due to another. This does not however reflect the scriptural, liturgical, or patristic language we see in Oriental Orthodoxy. For example, Athanasius, in his book *On the Incarnation*, is inclined to think of our debt as our death resulting from sin. Athanasius writes,

> "But since what was required from all still had to be rendered (for, as I said earlier, it was absolutely necessary to die and for this, in particular, he sojourned amongst us), for this reason, after the demonstration of his divinity from his works, he now offered the sacrifice on behalf of all, delivering his own temple to death in the stead of all, in order to make all not liable to and free from the ancient transgression, and to show himself superior to death, displaying his own body as

incorruptible, the first-fruits of the universal resurrection."[79]

The debt Athanasius speaks of here to be repaid is death which is the absence of life which came upon man because of the old trespass of Adam. This is echoed in the words of the sixth hour of the *Agpeya* (Coptic Book of Hours) where the litany says,

> "O You, Who on the sixth day and in the sixth hour was nailed to the cross, for the sin which our father Adam dared to commit in Paradise, tear the handwriting of our sins, O Christ our God, and save us."

There is clearly a debt and a handwriting of our sin, but Christ does not pay it in the sense of giving Himself in exchange for it. Rather, He ascends willingly to the cross and by subjecting Himself to the suffering and death of the cross, He tears the handwriting held against us and the death that comes with it. In this manner, Christ frees us or ransoms us having purchased us with His precious blood though without giving Satan and death anything as if He wished to satisfy them.

The language of ransom is used in the New Testament as early as the Gospel of Mark: "For even the Son of Man did not come to be served, but to serve, and to give His life a ransom for many" (Mark 10:45). It is easy to create all kinds of theories about what this ransom means when we are not familiar with the Old Testament, the original languages in which biblical texts are written, and the context in which

---

[79] Athanasius of Alexandria, *On the Incarnation of the Word*, (Yonkers: SVS Press), 93.

the audience of the text lived. For a brief background let us examine the following verse,

> "I am the Lord; I will bring you out from under the burdens of the Egyptians, I will rescue you from their bondage, and I will redeem you with an outstretched arm and with great judgments."
>
> Exodus 5:6

The root word used for "redeem" in the Septuagint is the same word used in Mark to refer to ransom. If we examine the Exodus narrative, God indeed redeems or ransoms the Israelites out of Egypt. God however is not seen paying a tribute to free the Israelites from the bondage of the Egyptians. Therefore, we do not have to think of Christ's ransom as payment of a physical tribute to Satan and death who are not worthy to receive anything from Christ. Thus, when we hear the priest praying the following passage in the Coptic Liturgy of Basil, "He loved his own who are in the world, and gave Himself up for our salvation unto death which reigned over us, whereby we were bound and sold on account of our sins," we do not have to think of Christ as paying anything to the devil but rather we ought to think of Him ransoming us out of Satanic and mortal bondage, setting free our race. The same language of debt payment by the Son to the Father is used by numerous Church Fathers in the East and West. It does not have to mean that the Father needed a tribute to free the humanity He loved to the extent of giving up His Son. Such an idea would be illogical and blasphemous as the Father, being God, is in need of nothing. We see in the patristic and liturgical traditions seemingly contradictory statements about the Son paying the debt of our sin to the Father—if not understood with correct Orthodox nuances. For example, we hear Gregory the Theologian in his second oration on Easter being opposed to this notion as he says,

> "We were detained in bondage by the Evil One, sold under sin, and receiving pleasure in exchange for wickedness. Now, since a ransom belongs only to him who holds in bondage, I ask to whom was this offered, and for what cause? If to the Evil One, fie upon the outrage! If the robber receives ransom, not only from God, but a ransom which consists of God Himself, and has such an illustrious payment for his tyranny, a payment for whose sake it would have been right for him to have left us alone altogether. But if to the Father, I ask first, how? For it was not by Him that we were being oppressed; and next, On what principle did the Blood of His Only begotten Son delight the Father, Who would not receive even Isaac, when he was being offered by his Father, but changed the sacrifice, putting a ram in the place of the human victim (Gen 22.11)? Is it not evident that the Father accepts Him, but neither asked for Him nor demanded Him; but on account of the Incarnation, and because Humanity must be sanctified by the Humanity of God, that He might deliver us Himself, and overcome the tyrant, and draw us to Himself by the mediation of His Son, Who also arranged this to the honor of the Father?"[80]

---

[80] Gregory Nazianzus, *Oration 45*, XXII.

It is obvious therefore that the sense in which the Son paid our debt to the Father was not one that was required to satisfy the wrath of the Father. The Father takes no pleasure in the shedding of blood and sacrifices but rather in the redemption of humanity from the tyranny of the devil. An Orthodox way of understanding the sacrifice of the Son being accepted by the Father comes from Cyril of Alexandria,

> "He freed nature from the bonds of death, and, once victorious, taught it to say, 'O death, where is your victory? O Hell, where is your sting? (Hos 13.14, 1 Cor 15.55)' And having made Heaven accessible to it through the economy of the Incarnation, he was taken up, presenting himself to the Father as the first-fruits of the human race."[81]

We can conclude this section by distinguishing two sides of the story of debt/ransom: there is an Orthodox story and an unorthodox story. The unorthodox story links the ransom to a physical payment being the blood of Christ which is paid to appease a wrathful and angry God or even worse, the devil. The Orthodox story links the debt to being under the dominion of death and sin and ransom to being rescued from this dominion through the death of Christ on the Cross. The result of understanding this model in an Orthodox way is that we no longer experience God as an angry being but rather as a loving Father who sends His Son for the salvation of humankind.

---

[81] "Festal Letter 1," Cyril of Alexandria, *Festal Letters 1-12*, (Washington D.C.: Catholic University of America Press, 2009), 51.

Sin

The fathers did not dedicate much of their time to speak about the nature of sin as their main concern was the eradication of sin and passions and the putting on of the new man in Christ. However, we are blessed with the writings of saints such as Athanasius, Cyril, and Severus who examined sin in the light of soteriology and salvation narrative. In Orthodox thinking, sin is not a substance, or a being created by God. God only creates what is good and sin is far from that. Sin is the free choice of human beings to submit themselves to a state of bondage that distances them from God. As such, Athanasius in his book *On the Incarnation of the Word* likens sin to darkness where both are nonbeing or the absence of being that is goodness or light. This is not said to compromise the gravity of sin. Rather, the purpose of this is to clarify that sin is not created by God but is rather the absence of goodness and that sin does not compromise the free will of man. Us being associated with Adam whose sin has real implications on our nature does not turn us into helpless creatures incapable of making their own decision whether to choose God (Being and Life), instead of sin (nonbeing and death). Our reality inherited from Adam entails an inclination to sin, corruption, and death; although none of these prevent us from attaining holiness through our reception of divine grace and our fellowship with the Trinity that becomes possible in Christ. Now, let us turn to the punitive dimension of sin.

Penalty/Punishment

There is a tendency in Orthodox circles to take on two extremes: deny any divine tendency to execute judgement or affirm that God is a punishing deity whose main task is to execute punitive judgement. The Orthodox Church takes a more moderate view of the consequence of sin being death. This section aims to answer the following questions: Who is executing the punishment? Who is pronouncing the punishment? Who is the recipient of punishment? What is the nature of the punishment? Let us begin with who was executing the punishment. The obvious answer might be God, but if it is, then how? Cyril, in his *Commentary on John* 1.9, answers this question,

> "Man then is a rational creature, but composite, of soul that is and of this perishable and earthly flesh. And when it had been made by God, and was brought into being, not having of its own nature incorruption and imperishableness (for these things appertain essentially to God Alone), it was sealed with the spirit of life, by participation with the Divinity gaining the good that is above nature (for He breathed, it says, into his nostrils the breath of life and man became a living soul). But when he was being punished for his transgressions, then rightly hearing Dust thou art and unto dust shalt thou return, he was bared of the grace; the breath of life, that is the Spirit of Him Who says I am the

Life, departed from the earthy body and the creature falls into death."[82]

This does not negate our role in bringing this punishment upon ourselves, as the Coptic Liturgy of Gregory the Theologian states, "But according to my will, I did eat. I put Your law behind me by my own counsel, and became slothful towards Your commandments. I plucked for myself the sentence of death." Later the same liturgy addresses Christ saying, "You have turned the punishment into salvation." In his *Oration 45*, Gregory also says,

> "And this was the first thing which he learned—his own shame—and he hid himself from God. Yet here too he makes a gain, namely death and the cutting off of sin, in order that evil may not be immortal. Thus, his punishment is changed into a mercy, for it is in mercy, I am persuaded, that God inflicts punishment."[83]

The nature of the punishment is not only merciful but also aims at our unity with Him as John Chrysostom puts it in his *Letter to Theodore*,

> "For if the wrath of God were a passion, one might well despair as being unable to quench the flame which he had kindled by so many evil doings; but since the Divine nature is passionless, even if He punishes, even if He takes vengeance, he does this not with wrath, but with tender care, and much loving-kindness; wherefore it behooves us to be of

---

[82] Cyril of Alexandria, *Commentary on John* (John 1.9), Vol. 1, *Library of Fathers of the Holy Catholic Church*, (London: James Parker & Co., 1874).

[83] Gregory Nazianzus, *Oration 45*, VIII.

much good courage, and to trust in the power of repentance. For even those who have sinned against Him He does not visit them with punishment for His own sake; for no harm can traverse that divine nature; but He acts with a view to our advantage, and to prevent our perverseness becoming worse by our making a practice of despising and neglecting Him... And for this reason, God threatens us with punishments, and often inflicts them, not as avenging Himself, but by way of attracting us to Himself."[84]

It is clear from the writings of the saints that the punishment is redemptive rather than vengeful. The purpose of all that God does for us, including punishment, is for our return and union with Him.

Substitution/Participation

The language of substitution between Christ and us is found throughout the writings of the Fathers and the Liturgical texts. For example, Gregory of Nyssa, in his commentary on the Lord's Prayer, writes,

> "The inclination of our free will was directed to slavery. The life of humans was subjugated by every evil. Death entered nature by a myriad of ways inasmuch as every suggestion of evil turns out to be a form of death against us. Therefore, because we have been entangled in this kind of tyranny and have been enslaved by death through evil passions which assault us like enemies and

---

[84] John Chrysostom, *Letter to Theodore Who Had Fallen*, 1.4.

executioners, it is good that we pray for God's Kingdom to come upon us. For by no other means can we put off the wicked subjugation of corruption except through the substitution of God's life-giving lordship over us. If we then ask that God's Kingdom should come upon us, we honestly entreat God to actualize in us these blessings: to be released from corruption; to be liberated from death, and to be loosed from the bonds of sin."[85]

The substitution here is between the dominion of death over us being substituted with the dominion of God in Christ over us. As such, the substitution is not a substitution of victims of divine wrath but rather it is a substitution of divine love and healing toward humankind manifested through divine dominion over us carried by the incarnation rendering the dominion of death over us powerless. The demolishing of the power of death comes through Christ becoming one of us and bestowing on us the presence of the Spirit whose life conquers our death. This is why the Coptic Friday Theotokion says, "He took what is ours and gave us what is His. He took our body and gave us His Holy Spirit." Gregory Nazianzus also says in his 83rd oration, "That which cannot be contained is contained… And He who gives riches becomes poor, for He assumes the poverty of my flesh, that I may assume the richness of His Godhead. He that is full empties Himself… that I may have a share in His fullness." The substitution as such is not limited to the cross neither is

---

[85] Gregory of Nyssa, *Homily III: On the Lord's Prayer* in St. Gregory of Nyssa, *Ancient Christian Writers, Vol. 18*, Hilda C. Graef (trans.), (New York: Paulist Press, 1954).

it a question of punishment but rather a question of divine generosity. Cyril extends the substitution language to the details of the life of Christ when he says in his *Apology against the Twelve Anathemas against Theodoret*,

> "He wept humanly to wipe your tears; and He feared economically letting His body succumb to what pertains to it that He may fill you with courage. In this manner, He became weak in His humanity that He might end your weakness; and He offers petitions and supplications to the Father to make the ear of the Father attentive to your prayers. As such, He took upon Himself all human weaknesses."[86]

The language of substitution, though canonical and evidently used by the Fathers, must be qualified with our participation and being in Christ. This participation is predicated on the common humanity between Christ and us since He assumed humanity like us in all things, save for sin alone. The Ethiopian Church in one of its Resurrection hymns says,

> "Through his flesh, he brought us close to him, after he had suffered in his flesh/… He who suffered, died and was buried, /vanquished death and rose from the dead! /Being a man, he was not alone in rising from the dead. /From of old, we know that he is the one whose divinity was known, /He conquered death by descending

---

[86] Cyril of Alexandria, Apology *Against the Twelve Anathemas Against Theodoret*, Patrologica Graeca 76:441 B, D.

> to Sheol in the flesh, he misled Satan by his appearance."[87]

The living and the dead alike are invited to participate in Christ and realize their place in Him as ones rising with the Crucified and Risen Christ. Indeed, only Christ dies on the Cross, but we are not alien to the sacrifice of the Cross. As Cyril puts it in his *Commentary on John* 1:29,

> "For when we were guilty of many sins, and for that reason were liable to death and destruction, the Father gave His Son a ransom for us, one for all, since all are in Him, and He is greater than all. One died for all, that we all might live in him: Death devoured the Lamb on behalf of all, and then vomited all in Him, and with Him. For we were all in Christ, who died and rose again on our account on our behalf."[88]

Our Lord endured suffering alone yet He allows us to suffer with Him as Paul said,

> "Yet indeed I also count all things loss for the excellence of the knowledge of Christ Jesus my Lord, for whom I have suffered the loss of all things, and count them as rubbish, that I may gain Christ and be found in Him, not having my own righteousness, which is from the law, but that which is through faith in Christ, the righteousness

---

[87] Emmanuel Fritsch, The Liturgical Year of the Ethiopian Church: The Temporal: Seasons and Sundays, *Ethiopian review of cultures* v. 9-10 (2001), 242.

[88] Cyril of Alexandria, *Commentary on John* (John 1.29) Vol. 1, in Joel C. Elowsky, (ed.), David R. Maxwell (trans.), *Ancient Christian Texts: Cyril of Alexandria*, (Downers Grove: InterVarsity Press, 2013).

which is from God by faith; that I may know Him and the power of His resurrection, and the fellowship of His sufferings, being conformed to His death, if, by any means, I may attain to the resurrection from the dead."

Philippians 3:8-11

We are always invited to be with Christ and in Christ through the Spirit whose work in the Church allows us to become partakers of the divine nature, fellows with God and recipients of His grace.

The Victorious Sacrifice

Having covered the various ways one can speak of the salvation Christ offered whether through debt and ransom, substitution and participation, or through the language of punishment and justice, it is time to turn to the twofold model of salvation through Christ, the Victim and Victor. There is a modern inclination to uphold one over the other. The Church however teaches a balance between the two extremes where Christ is always the sacrificial victim who gives Himself up for the life of the world while always acknowledging Him as the victorious conqueror of the principalities of death. Like other models explaining the salvation Christ offered, it should not be solely seen in the light of the crucifixion but in the light of the total salvific work of Christ beginning with His conception to His ascension and beyond. Let us use the temptation on the Mount as an example; Christ is subjecting Himself to be in a sense a victim of demonic temptation yet at the same time, He, bearing us within Him, conquers Satan and his temptations. On the Cross, Christ subjects Himself to suffering and death as a victim of state and religious justice systems. However, Paul describes the work of Christ on the Cross as the work of a victorious conqueror who "having wiped out the handwriting of requirements that was against us, which was contrary to us. And He has taken it out of the way, having nailed it to the cross. Having disarmed principalities and powers, He made a public spectacle of them, triumphing over them in it" (Colossians 2:14-15).

Christ is conqueror even in offering Himself to the Father as an acceptable sacrifice. In His descent into Hades, He, being dead as man, identifies with the dead who are chained with death, yet He emerges victorious having freed those who have accepted His preaching who awaited the promise of His coming. In the Resurrection, He is evidently victorious over death and hades, yet He bears the mark of His sacrifice in the marks of the wounds on His body. Icons of the Resurrection, though they focus on the victory of Christ over death, depict Christ holding the banner of the resurrection with a cross on it and with His hands and feet having the marks of the wounds. Even in His ascension into glory where He lifted up our human nature to be seated at the right hand of the Father, Christ continues to bear the marks of His sufferings which Cyril describes in a dramatic fashion in his *Commentary on John*,

> "He says, 'Who is This That cometh from Edom, with dyed garments from Bosra?' They who raise this shout, I mean the cry, 'Who is This That cometh from Edom? that is, from the earth, are angels and rational powers, for they are marveling

at the Lord ascending into heaven.' And, seeing Him almost, as it were, dyed in His own Blood, they say unto Him, not yet apprehending the mystery, 'Why is Your apparel red, and why are Your garments like him that treads in the wine-vats? For they compare the color of the blood to new wine, lately trodden in the press. And what does Christ say unto them? First, in order that He may be known to be the living God, He says, 'I speak righteousness; using the word speak, instead of 'teach.'' And most assuredly, He that teaches righteousness must be a Lawgiver, and if a Lawgiver, then surely also God. Then the angels say unto Him, as Christ shows them the marks of the nails, 'What are these wounds in Your Hands?' and the Lord answers, 'Those with which I was wounded in the house of My beloved…'"[89]

Throughout His life on earth, Christ's sacrificial character is seen as He willingly submits to the human condition and in doing so, He emerges victorious having won the good fight for us who have failed to win against the temptations posed before us throughout our lives beginning with the fall of Adam and Eve to our own personal failings. In Him, we see the victory of the lamb and the humility of the lion. Upon Him our paradoxical salvation rests as He heals humanity while He lifts up the curse of the law by becoming a curse; He accepts sufferings by His own will

---

[89] Cyril of Alexandria, *Commentary on John* (John 20.27) in Joel C. Elowsky (ed.), David R. Maxwell (trans.), *Ancient Christian Texts: Cyril of Alexandria's Commentary on John*, Vol. 2, (Downers Grove: InterVarsity Press, 2015).

while He offers us a new victorious beginning; He ransoms us yet He pays Satan and death nothing; He takes our place yet He allows us to partake in Him through the sacramental life of the Church, His body. Let us conclude with the Armenian Ode for the Ascension of Christ God by Gregory Narek,

> "The fallen nature he renewed through His resurrection, raising it with Himself unto glory, seating it on the throne of glory in the highest realm. The King of Glory arise to do battle; He took captive the one who takes captives. Ascending high, He distributed gifts to human beings. In human body, with the color of blood, the incorporeal Lord was sighted by angels."[90]

Knit to the Godhead

When Christ became one of us, His work was to return us once more to the fellowship of the Holy Trinity, or to use the words of Athanasius in the third discourse of *Against the Arians*, "we have become knit into the Godhead."[91] The sacramental life of the Church performs this role of knitting us into the Godhead through God giving us Himself through tangible matter. Christ's incarnation sanctified all matter making the use of matter to communicate the life of God to us a possibility. As such, water is used in baptism to aid us in putting off the old man, dying, and burying ourselves under water, rising with Christ, and putting on Christ.

---

[90] Abraham Terian, *The Festal Works of St. Gregory of Narek: Annotated Translation of the Odes, Litanies, and Encomia*, 2016, 73.

[91] Athanasius of Alexandria, *Against the Arians*, 3.24.

Through oil, we receive the gift and fellowship of the Spirit. Through crowns made of flowers, olive branches, or metal, men and women come into a marital union sanctioned by the Spirit. Through bread and wine, we receive the body and blood of Christ having become members of His body. All the previous models that explain our salvation point to the reality that all that Christ did for us was motivated by His love for the sake of the redemption, healing and deification of our human nature. Sacraments and the entirety of the life of the Church become the path toward our highest calling of human healing, namely our deification.

Deification

> *"O Lord, when my soul was annihilated from the tree of life, You gave me deification and made me one with You."*
>
> –Coptic Orthodox Fraction of Nativity

+ + +

God blessed man by calling him to be deified through living in eternal communion with Him enjoying the light of His divine glory. We have been called to become "partakers of the divine nature having escaped the corruption in the world caused by evil desires" (2 Peter 1:4). We are called to become godlike not due to our own goodness. Rather, it is because we have been called and blessed by God with grace and faith that aid us in doing good works by which we glorify our Father in heaven. Deification is a God given grace to those who have emptied themselves with Him and have been crucified with Him that they may be glorified with Christ.

Christ said, "And the glory which You gave Me I have given them, that they may be one just as We are one" (John 17:22). Therefore, deification may be seen as a double unity: unity of God with humans and unity of humans among themselves. The fruits of deification are adoption to God the Father through His Son in the Holy Spirit, a life of imitating Christ, a state of repentance, co-suffering with Christ, and becoming co-glorified with Him. We must never forget that there is no deification (or *theopoesis, theosis*, etc.) apart from self-emptying (or *kenosis*). The ultimate reception of deification takes place after our departure from this world, though its fruits begin the day we are baptized and continue as we continue to acquire the Holy Spirit and partake of the Eucharist. The early Church expressed her faith in deification in numerous ways through Church fathers and divine Liturgies which we will examine together throughout this chapter.

"God has become man that man might become god" is a phrase commonly repeated by many fathers in different variations. The key to understand the term "become" in relation to our deification is deeply rooted in our understanding of the same term in relation to Christology. If we understand how God "became" man, it will be significantly easier to understand how man "becomes" god. Today, the word "become" is often used to signify a change from one substance to another. Theologically, the use of the term differs drastically. In Christology, "become" cannot signify change as Christ, being God by nature, is not susceptible to change. Instead, the Word "becoming" flesh signifies the Word uniting Himself to mortal flesh, making it His own. It is therefore logically consistent to understand the second "become" in the phrase in the same manner we understood the first. Our "becoming" god does not signify an ontological change but rather a unity with the divine. The first unity differs however from the second in that the first unity is a natural unity in which the divinity and humanity are coming together in the composite hypostasis of Christ. The second unity between us and God is a unity of grace and love, resembling that which is between a man and his wife, given to us by the Father in the Son through the Spirit. The distinction between these two modes of unity is described by Severus of Antioch in his work *Against the Grammarian*,

> "The only begotten Son of God became consubstantial with us by being united hypostatically to one flesh animated with a rational soul. By reason of this, the entire human *ousia* and the whole race became united in love to the divine nature from which it had formally been estranged. Hence, as it is written, we being made worthy of the original harmony, have become partakers of the divine nature."[92]

The Patristic Witness

The fathers speak of deification in multiple ways such as illumination, adoption, union with God, indwelling of the

---

[92] Severus of Antioch, *Contra Impium Grammaticum* I, in V.C. Samuel, *The Council of Chalcedon Re-Examined: A History and Theological Survey*, (Madras: Christian Literature Society for the Senate of Serampore College, 1977), 235.

Spirit, and glorification, etc. The language of illumination and light is seen in the writings of theologians like Gregory Nazianzus who lived as early as the fourth century. Gregory says in an *Oration on the Holy Lights*,

> "The light shines in darkness, in this life and in the flesh, and is chased by the darkness but is not overtaken by it. By this I mean the adverse power leaping up in its shamelessness again the visible Adam but encountering God and being defeated—in order that we, putting away the darkness, may draw near the Light and may then become perfect Light, the children of perfect Light."[93]

Christians are called to become perfect Light and children of perfect Light. The incarnation of the Son is the shining of His light in our darkness and because His light is far greater than our darkness, we become light inasmuch as we receive His light. Although He is perfect light and we become perfect light, there remains a gap between God as the illuminating Light and us as the ones illuminated by His light. Cyril explains this difference in his *Commentary on the Gospel of John* where he writes,

> "It is one thing to enlighten and another to be enlightened. One is active; the other is passive. The Son enlightens, and the creation is enlightened. Therefore, the Son and creation are not the same

---

[93] Gregory of Nazianzus, *Oration 39*, II.

since that which acts is not the same as that which is acted on."[94]

Our deification is then explained by Cyril in the following terms in the same commentary,

> "We were all in Christ, and the shared properties of our human nature were taken up into his person. That is why he is called the last Adam. He gives all the riches of his tranquility and glory to our common nature, just as the first Adam gave us corruption and shame. Therefore, the Word "dwelt in" all people through the one man so that when the one man 'was designated Son of God in power according to the Spirit of holiness," this honor might extend to all humanity. In this way, because of one of us, the words, 'I said that you are gods, and you are all sons of the Most High' might come to us as well. Therefore, the slave is truly freed in Christ and ascends into mystical unity with the one who bore the form of a slave, while at the same time Christ is in us in the sense that we are like him because of our kinship with his flesh"[95]

Our adoption to the Father in Christ is another way the fathers speak of deification. Their thoughts are best summarized by Patriarch Timothy II Aelurus who says,

---

[94] See Joel C. Elowsky (ed.), David R. Maxwell (trans.), *Ancient Christian Texts: Cyril of Alexandria's Commentary on John*, Vol. 2, (Downers Grove: InterVarsity Press, 2015).

[95] Cyril of Alexandria, *Commentary on John* (John 1.14) in Joel C. Elowsky (ed.), David R. Maxwell (trans.), *Ancient Christian Texts: Cyril of Alexandria's Commentary on John*, Vol. 1, (Downers Grove: InterVarsity Press, 2013), 64.

> "[The Son] became like us, by the providence of God, so that we might become like him because of his loving kindness. He became man, without abandoning his being Son of God, in order that we might, through the grace of God, become sons of God."[96]

Severus of Antioch, in his *18th Homily*, uses the language of light as well in describing the illumination of the martyrs who received the light prior to their departure to the heavenly realm,

> "From heaven, the Master of the Games watched them, while at the same time a choir of angels rejoiced, and prepared to meet them, and rehearsed hymns of victory for the athletes. And a light, descending from on high, picked out and illuminated the stadium of their contest, similar to that light which our Lord showed on the mountain to the disciples, when *his face shone like the sun and his clothes became white as lights* (Matt 17:2), for he loves to glorify his true servants like himself."[97]

The Coptic and Syriac fathers in the medieval era did not deviate from the ethos of the fathers of the patristic age. Bulus Al-Bushi, a thirteenth century Copto-Arab theologian and Bishop, writes the following in a homily on the feast of Annunciation,

---

[96] R.Y. Ebeid and L.R. Wickham, "A Collection of Unpublished Syriac Letters of Timothy Aelurus," *Journal of Theological Studies* 21, no. 2 (October 1970): 360.

[97] Pauline Allen and C. T. R. Hayward, *Severus of Antioch*, (London: Routledge, 2005), 122.

"Thus, the joy of today's noble feast is a general annunciation to the whole world, for it declares to us the coming of the Lord, and the unity of His imperceptible divinity to our weak perishing nature, until He strengthened it and made it victorious over death and triumphant over Satan and his hosts."[98]

In another *Homily on the Feast of Nativity*, Bulus stresses our unity with God in the following terms,

"Let us keep our souls pure from evil thought, for the sake of the reverence of Him who was united to our body, that He might bring us closer to the eternal and imperceptible glory of His divinity. Let us keep our senses untarnished by disgrace, for the sake of the honour of Him who has purified humanity's body, soul and mind, through His union with it. And because of His great and uncontainable humanity, He did not shy away from calling us His brethren as it is written, 'I will proclaim Your name to my brothers.'"[99]

Ibn El-Makin was another Coptic theologian of the thirteenth century who wrote in his book *Al-Hawi* that

"It is impossible for deified humans and angels near Him to delight in beholding the transcendent

---

[98] Manqarious Awadallah (ed.), *Maqalat Bulus Al-Bushi Osqof Misr w A'maluha* (*The Articles of Paul of Bush, Bishop of Egypt*), 12. Translated by the author.
[99] Manqarious Awadallah, *Maqalat Bulus Al-Bushi*, 34-35.

essence of His divinity for all created beings are prevented from that."[100]

As such, Ibn El-Makin recognizes that our deification does not compromise the full transcendence of the unapproachable essence of God. On the Syriac front, Bar Hebraeus in his book *The Ethikon* presents deification in the light of the mind that is united with God through prayer and asceticism. Bar Hebraeus writes,

> "the chained minds, upon beholding a deified mind, they shiver with desire to walk along with Him, be united with Him, wish to not be separated from Him, and rejoice in Him."[101]

Bar Hebraeus, drawing on the fathers who preceded him, gives the following analogy,

> "Contemplate the iron united to fire. You do not distinguish then the characteristics of the iron for it has been changed by its unity with the fire. As such, you no longer see two forms but one form. However, the essential physical properties are preserved in each. In this manner, the children of God see themselves in the light of seeing their Lord

---

[100] Al-Makin Jirgis Ibn Al-'amid Al-Saghir, *Al-Hawi (The Collective)* published by Tawadrous Al-Shahat (Hegomen) and Fouad Bassily, 29-30. Translated by the author.

[101] Gregorios Bar Hebraeus, *Ethikon* (Qamishli, Syria: Shaffir), 2001. retrieved from https://dss-syriacpatriarchate.org. Translated by the author.

that they may all be deified because of the grace and generosity of their Lord."[102]

There are countless other examples of the sayings of the fathers who uphold the doctrine of deification as the greatest vocation of man, but I believe the excerpts quoted in this chapter suffice. Evidently, the doctrine of deification is central to the Christian faith as seen in the scripture where Peter declares humans as "partakers of the divine nature," the fathers of the universal Church and the fathers of the Oriental Orthodox Church in the medieval era. The liturgical life of our Church as well leaves no chance without declaring our potential deification in Christ as we will see below.

The Liturgical Dimension

The Liturgical life of the Church is the best expression of her faith as we believe and live what we pray. Metropolitan Mor Isaac Sakka believes the Liturgy to be the unfailing project of deification as he writes in his commentary on the Syriac Orthodox Liturgy,

> "the project of deification man has planned (you will become like God) was a failing project. As for the project [of deification] planned by Jesus Christ, it was a successful project."[103]

Through the Liturgy, our eating of the fruit of the tree of knowledge to be deified apart from God is undone by the

---

[102] Gregorios Bar Hebraeus, Ethikon (Qamishli, Syria: Shaffir), 2001 retrieved from https://dss-syriacpatriarchate.org. Translated by the author.
[103] Ishaq Sakka, 26.

bread and wine that become the body and blood which deify us in God.

Just as the language of light is prevalent throughout the writings of the Fathers, it is likewise seen in the Syriac Liturgy. The Orthodox congregants in the Syriac Church chant the opening hymn which announces the beginning of the divine Liturgy with the following words,

> "By thy light shall we see the light, Jesus full of light. Thou, True Light, gives the light to your creatures all. Lighten us with Your bright light, You, the Father's Light Divine. Thou who dwellest in the light-mansions, holy, pure; keep us from all hateful thoughts, from all passions vile. Grant us cleanness in our hearts; deeds of righteousness to do."

The Liturgy is the place of our illumination with the true light of Jesus Christ who cleanses our hearts from defilement and introduces righteousness into our souls. The rootedness of deification in the incarnation of the Son is seen vividly in the Anaphora of Jacob of Serug where the presbyter prays,

> "He became man of His own will in order to make us gods as it pleased Him. He was born of the womb of flesh that He might bring us forth from the spiritual womb."

The Syriac prayer for the Feast of Pentecost portrays deification as a union and mingling with Christ God: "O Christ, our God, unite us through our mingling with You."

The Friday midnight prayer of the Coptic Church alludes to deification as a mutual participation between us and Christ as it says, "He took our body and gave us His Holy Spirit, and made us one with Him through His goodness." Coptic Divine Liturgies end with a seasonal prayer known as the fraction. In one of those fractions known as the fraction of the lamb of God, the presbyter says, "Make us worthy of the coming down of Your Holy Spirit in our souls... let Your Spirit dwell within us." The Ethiopian Liturgy refers to deification as a mixture between us and God similar to the mixing of wine and water in the chalice. As the presbyter mixes the water and wine, he prays the following passage from the Anaphora of the Son of Thunder,

> "As with the mixture of this wine with water, the one cannot be separated from the other, so let thy divinity be united with our humanity, and our humanity with thy divinity, and let thy greatness be united with our humility and our humility with thy greatness."

Mary: A Model for Humanity

Various Oriental Orthodox Churches have shown their love to Mary, the Mother of God, in various ways. The Copts dedicate the month of Kiahk (this month ends with the Coptic commemoration of Nativity) to praise her life, her dedication to God and her role in the incarnation. The Ethiopians read the *Miracles of Mary* at the end of every Liturgy. Recently, the Syrians use the feast of the dormition of the Theotokos in the lands of immigration to gather all Syriac believers within a given demographic in one parish where they can celebrate the feast in unison. The Armenians, under the guidance of Karekin I Catholicos of All Armenia, began dedicating the feast of the annunciation to Mary as the day of Motherhood and blessing of all families. In a sense, Mary has become a uniting person who gathers all Oriental Orthodox believers around love and dedication to her exemplary life.

In Orthodoxy, Mary is not a great exception but rather a great example. Orthodox Christianity does not subscribe to doctrines such as the immaculate conception or coronation of Mary that distance Mary from the rest of us. Rather, we believe her to be the simple girl whose humility made her worthy before God to receive in her womb the Son of God who was to form His humanity from her body by the power of the Most High overshadowing her and the Spirit coming on her. We do not know much about her life from the canonical Gospels except for a few occasions in relation to Christ. In this chapter, I hope to share with you some of what we can learn about the Theotokos from the little we know about her life from the Gospels and tradition.

The tradition of the Church teaches that Mary's parents Joachim and Anna were barren and that their barrenness was a cause of shame given the context they lived in. Joachim left Anna and retreated to the desert for prayer that God may remove their shame. He was reassured in a vision that he would have a daughter. The story of Joachim and Anna can be a source of hope and guidance for those struggling with infertility. The role of Joachim who turned shame into prayer is another invaluable lesson a Christian can learn from the story of the conception of the Theotokos. After Mary was born, her parents dedicated her to the temple from a very young age. Dedicating our children to the Lord whether in a parent-child context or a priest-spiritual child context is another lesson one can learn from Mary's parents. In the secular age we live in, it is easy for parents to lose sight of their primary role as guides for their children toward eternal life and focus on their children's academic and financial life. Evidently, this was not the priority of Joachim and Anna.

Mary's humility and submission to the voice of the angel is a lesson in fulfilling God's callings for us. Our vows of monasticism, marriage, priesthood, and consecration are all ways of responding to the divine call for all human beings to become saints. On the path towards saintliness, one ought to be vigilant and watchful just as Mary was when she witnessed the events concerning the birth of Christ and kept it all within her heart. John Chrysostom attributes the incidents of losing Jesus at the temple and Mary pushing Christ before His time to perform a miracle at the wedding at Cana to the human weakness of Mary. These weaknesses help us realize that even the holiest human being after Christ, who was fully divine and fully human, has succumbed to weakness. This gives us hope in attaining holiness in spite of our weaknesses.

The final scene in which Mary appears in the Gospels is under the foot of the Cross witnessing the excruciating suffering and execution of her only Son Jesus Christ. The litany of the ninth hour of the *Agpeya* (Coptic Book of Hours) describe this scene in the following words,

"When the mother saw the lamb and the shepherd of the whole world hung on the cross, she said while weeping, 'The world rejoices at receiving salvation but my heart aches as I behold your crucifixion which you are enduring for the sake of all my Son and my God."

Her patient endurance is certainly a model that Christians, who are like a dough baked with the fire of suffering, can follow.

The events of the death and dormition of the Theotokos are engraved in the tradition of the Church though they are not recorded in the New Testament. The presence of Christ who receives her pure soul and the angels carrying her body to heavens while her robe is entrusted to Thomas are attested to in the ancient iconography of the Church. An icon in the Monastery of St. Mary Al-Suryan in Egypt depicts Christ carrying the soul of the Mother of God in the form of a child can be a window of contemplation as we behold Christ holding her in the form of a child just as she held him in her arms as a child. This is echoed in the words of the Coptic midnight praises, "He took what is ours and gave us what is His." This language of exchange in iconography and hymnography is seen in its most vivid form in the mystery of the Mother of God who becomes our mother since the moment the crucified Christ says to her regarding the beloved disciple and all of us, "Behold your child." We have a fellowship with John enjoying her motherhood and her example as the one who became like Christ in as much as that is humanly possible to the extent that Orthodox believers call her the most holy.

In the physical ascension of her body into heavens after death, we hope and pray that our souls may start ascending toward God both now and beyond this life. In our quest for becoming an icon of Christ, we can hope with Gregory of Nyssa that Christ may be formed within us day by day spiritually in the heart just as he was formed within the Theotokos physically in the womb.

Chapter 8

Orthodox Worship and Prayer

"True holiness is achieved by the combination of hope, faith and love expressed in worship and daily life. Give your strength and time to prayer and worship and the loving service of your fellowmen, and the passions will gradually be conquered."[104]

—*Metropolitan Paulos Mar Gregorios*

+++

Orthodox worship is deeply rooted in the theology of the Trinity, the incarnation and the sacramental life of the Church. Worship is always directed to the Trinity whom we come in communication with through the sacramental life of the Church beginning with baptism by which we can call the Father, "Abba Father," have allegiance with the Son as "the firstborn brother," and be filled with the Holy Spirit. Coptic Bishop Poemen of Malawi comments on the trinitarian form of worship saying,

> "In every prayer or service, Orthodoxy emphasizes the work of the three persons of the Trinity... We find the priest give the Apostolic blessing saying, 'The love of God the Father, the grace of the Only

---

[104] Paulos Gregorios, *The Kingdom of "Diakonia,"* (Kottayam, India: Mar Gregorios Foundation, 2014), 30.

begotten Son and the communion, gift and fellowship of the Holy Spirit be with all.' In the *Agpeya* [Coptic Book of Hours] prayers, 'We thank you O Father, the Father of our Lord, God and Savior Jesus Christ' and then another similar prayer is offered to the Son. There is a Liturgy that is directed to the Father and another liturgy directed to the Son. The Orthodox Church teaches that the three persons of the Trinity work in the unity of the essence of love."[105]

The incarnation informs our mode of prayer as the second Person of the Trinity became man, He assumed all that belongs to our humanity apart from sin. Therefore, all that He assumed is now capable of being healed and attaining deification. Orthodox worship as such involves the entirety of our being: bodily, rational, and spiritual worship. In beholding Christ, Orthodox Christians see the One who spent the night keeping vigils (Luke 6:12) and praying for unity first and foremost (John 17). In beholding the Theotokos, Orthodox Christians are reminded to combine their worship with a meditation and a constant remembrance of the details of the life of Christ emulating her who kept Christ's life in her heart (Luke 2:19, 51). Orthodox Christians unite their mind with its understanding to their spirit that longs for God, as it is written, "I will pray with my spirit, but I will also pray with my understanding; I will sing with my spirit, but I will also sing with my understanding" (1 Cor. 14:15). Simultaneously, Paul exhorts his disciple

---

[105] Bishop Poemen, *Two Articles on Orthodox Spirituality*, (Cairo: al-Mahaba Printing Press), 70.

Timothy to engage his body in prayer saying, "Therefore I want the men in every place to pray, lifting up holy hands, without wrath and dissension" (1 Tim. 2: 8).

An Orthodox prayer life engages the body, soul, mind, thoughts, heart, emotions, and feelings in uniting with God. One cannot attend an authentic prayerful life apart from repentance. As one reveals what is lacking within their soul to the Lord, the Lord in turn reveals His holiness to the praying person that they may be able to leave their passions behind and further long for divine likeness. As Mor Gregorios Thirumeni of the Malankara Orthodox Church puts it,

> "Prayer is one thing, which can help education to develop faith, devotion and mutual good will among people. He who prayers to God everyday will never be untrue, evil, faithless, an enemy of society or a traitor... Prayer is the enthusiasm of childhood, the refuge of youth, and peace in old age. God will listen to the prayer of a heart full of devotion and such a person will get abundant blessings from God in return. A real devotee of God is one who selflessly loves all his fellow-beings, because God has created everything as the object of our love. More things are wrought by prayer than we can even dream of. How can we say that man is better than we can ever dream of. How can we say that man is better than animals, which cannot discern their future, if even after knowing. God, man does not raise his hand in prayer, for his own sake and also for the sake of those whom he loves? Prayer, thus is golden chain by which we are

bound to the holy feet of God. Therefore, pray earnestly to God, day and night. Such prayer is the best means to remove the darkness in us, to free us from fatigue, to accomplish our needs and it can lead us to salvation and Heaven. Believe in God and pray to Him; my brethren, God will be pleased in you!"[106]

Fr. Mathew the Poor, a Coptic monk who discipled many monks and lived for a while in solitude, authored a book called *Orthodox Prayer Life* in which he outlined the various stages of prayer. In his *Orthodox Prayer Life*, Fr. Matthew writes,

"Prayer that is spiritual and genuine is both a call and a response: a divine call and a human response. This definition of prayer rests on an important fact: Prayer does not reach its power and efficacy as an actual communion with God until man is fully aware that his soul is created in God's image. He should feel that it derives its very being from him. In this being, nothing is more vital than this self-awareness. Once man's soul becomes sure of this, it will have laid hold of the source of such awareness—which is God. Thus, the soul realizes, sees, and touches God's self."[107]

Prayer as such is a movement from Adam the first in whom we died toward Adam the second, Christ, in whom Life is bestowed upon us. The incarnation is not limited to

---

[106]Mor Gregorios Thirumeni as quoted in *Biography of Parumala Thirumeni* by P. N. Chacko, 35-38.

[107] Matthew the Poor, *Orthodox Prayer Life: The Interior Way*, (Yonkers: SVS Press, 2003), 21.

that vertical movement from earthliness in Adam to the heavenliness of Christ but is extended to encompass the horizontal and communal movement of the Christian in communion with other believers. Bishop Poemen in his article "Orthodox Spirituality" writes,

> "If we contemplate the Liturgy, we will behold this unity [of believers] in a vivid manner as the bishop on his own cannot celebrate a Liturgy neither can a deacon alone nor the congregation without the bishop and deacon."[108]

Furthermore, this unity of believers in prayer surpasses the boundaries of death. Bishop Poemen writes,

> "the strong bond between the triumphant consummated in the faith with the struggling who continuously run toward salvation is an essential dimension of Orthodox spirituality."[109]

Thus, it is common for the Orthodox Church to dedicate prayers for the dead and ask for their prayers.

Orthodox prayer utilizes the presence of matter in the world for the salvation of humankind. This is founded on the incarnation being the unity of divinity with humanity which includes the physical matter of which our bodies are made. Bishop Poemen writes in this regard,

> "The Church considers matter a necessary element of the work of God for the salvation of man. Since the Son, the Word, received the nature of man in

---

[108] Bishop Poemen, *Two Articles*, 72.
[109] Bishop Poemen, *Two Articles*, 72.

His hypostasis having united divinity with humanity, matter is no longer considered unclean but rather a blessed dimension and a medium through which the Church offers the grace and gifts of the Spirit. Water, oil, bread and wine are necessary mediums for the reception of the sacraments of the Church... Our bodies themselves will resurrect in glory when the Lord comes in His glory and the glory of His Father, for we are the children of the light, the children of the Resurrection. The bodies of saints will be illuminated with light and glory after the resurrection and the body itself will partake with the soul in the blessings of the age to come as it partook with it in the labors of the world. Orthodoxy even believes that the realm of created matter will be glorified with the resurrection of man and the glorification of his body. For just as matter was corrupted and polluted with the corruption of man, the priest of creation, likewise it will be glorified when he is glorified. In this regard, Paul the apostle says, 'For we know that the whole creation groans and labors with birth pangs together until now. Not only that, but we also who have the first fruits of the Spirit, even we ourselves groan within ourselves, eagerly waiting for the adoption, the redemption of our body' (Romans 8: 22-23)."[110]

Therefore, Orthodox believers venerate icons and use them in their churches and prayer corners. Similarly, they use musical instruments in the liturgical life of the Church that

---

[110] Bishop Poemen, *Two Articles,* 74-75.

reflect the beauty of worship. The Armenians use the organ; the Copts use the cymbal and triangle; the Ethiopians and Eritreans use drums and the staff of Yared; few Syriac and Malankara parishes use the organ. The use of music is utilized to reflect the ethos of each Church and to add an element of beauty. This is not to be confused with the use of music to manipulate the emotions of those engaged in prayer. Thus, the various Oriental Orthodox Churches have often warned through sermons, and synodal decrees against the use of evangelical Christian music within Orthodox Churches as the purpose of using musical instruments and the ethos differs rather drastically. In the Orthodox context, icons and instruments are meant to aid the believers in engaging, not manipulating all their senses in the journey of prayer toward a real, not solely emotional, union with God.

The soul is like a dove flying with the wings of communal prayer and personal prayer toward union with God. Oftentimes, one commits to an element without the other based on their preference or their personality as to whether they are introverted or extroverted. The struggle is to attain a balance between the communal and the personal. This struggle is not one that is overcome in a day or two but rather takes a lifetime to develop. A life of prayer is a life of continuous growth in knowledge of the Infinite. Therefore, one can imagine that there is no point in which one can say, "I have attained a life of prayer." There is always room for growth. As Orthodox Christians, we are graced with numerous fathers who shed light on the path of prayer.

Paulos Mar Gregorios offers the following advice to Christians aiming to develop a life of prayer,

> "The **first rule** in prayer as in swimming, is not to give up just because you do not succeed in the first three or four attempts. Prayer is a spiritual skill to be acquired by constant practice. The **second rule**, again as in swimming is to 'let go,' to let the water support you, to be unanxious and relaxed. In prayer also we have to let ourselves go, relax, trust in God to support you and teach you how to pray. The **third rule** is to keep up the practice, even if you do not feel like it, or enjoy it. In the life of prayer, our inherent love of sensual pleasures and our selfish love of laziness and comfort, will interfere to make us reluctant to keep up the practice, finding various excuses for not praying. There is no use saying, 'I don't feel like praying' or, 'I do not get anything from it.' It will take years before you get the habit of prayer and really begin to enjoy it. One must strengthen the will to have control over the laziness of the body and the desires of the flesh if one is to make progress in the art and skill of prayer. There is nothing like regular practice which can teach you to pray. A **fourth rule**, closely connected with the third, is: develop the discipline of prayer through fasting and self-control. Man does not become free and good like God until he learns to control his own inner drives and passions. Restraint of hunger and thirst, of anger and jealousy, of sexual passion, of the desire for glory and flattery, of the desire for bodily excitement and for sensual stimulation, and of all inner turbulences which make us do things against our own free will, is a necessary

preparation for prayer. As good athletes competing for the Olympic Games go through very rigorous self-discipline in order to keep their body, muscles and nerves in good condition, so should the man of prayer keep his body, mind and spirit and good condition and under conscious control. A **fifth rule** is to use our whole body and even material things in the service of prayer. Prayer is an act of the whole man, body, soul and spirit—not simply an act of the mind. The body can participate in prayer through posture, speech, and acts."[111]

Applying these rules is a good start for our journey of prayer that is holistic, communal, and personal aiming toward union with God. Gregory Bar Hebraeus in his book *The Ethicon* shares six marks of perfect prayer that Christians should aspire to attain,

"The **first** and greatest work is the purity of the thoughts. Regarding this says Mor Isaac, 'Pure and perfect prayer is not only offered with an undisturbed mind but even with a mind that is distant from the memory of what is meaningless. Even more there is no room for meaningless thoughts in such mind which can cause a disturbance. The **second** is to understand the sentences you utter in prayer. He who does not know what he says, it is better for him to remain silent. The **third** is to cultivate an inner awareness of the greatness of the Lord. The wisdom behind this is twofold: first, that man may dwell on the greatness of God while he stands before him in

---

[111] Paulos Mar Gregorios., *Prayer Book for Young People*, (Kottayam: Sophia Publications, 1978), 8-10.

prayer, and second, is to understand the weakness of the nature of the one praying. When an elder was contemplating these two matters, he used to say before God inaudibly: how can I contemplate you O Lord while you know that I am foolish and know nothing. You brought me to existence. Therefore, save me because of your mercy for I am a servant and the son of a maidservant who is nothing but dust and ashes. These two things are what the Mother of God herself said while her soul magnified the Mighty and Holy name of the Lord who beheld the weakness of His maidservant. The **fourth** is the reverence resulting from the knowledge of the greatness and might of God. Thus, Evagrius says, 'Prayer is indeed obsolete and useless if it is a plead without reverence, purity, and watchfulness. Thus, the demons whisper their ideas to carry the mind away rendering it empty, dysfunctional, and unable to benefit from prayer to the Lord. The **fifth** is the shame that man experiences upon the remembrance of his sins and trespasses. As such, one calls upon Him and says, 'I have sinned against heaven and before you and am not worthy to be called your son.' The **sixth** is the hope resulting from our knowledge of God's compassion and containment of every being. When hope grows, it gives birth to the indescribable joy of the soul."[112]

---

[112] Gregorios Bar Hebraeus, *Ethikon* (Qamishli: Shaffir, 2001) retrieved from https://dss-syriacpatriarchate.org/ and translated by the author.

These rules and guidelines can be difficult to follow but our struggles are leavened with the grace of the Spirit who vivifies our spiritual life that we may attain union with God.

Orthodox worship continues beyond the communal and personal prayer when one's entire being becomes engaged with prayer as the Psalmist says, "I give myself to prayer" (Psalm 109:4). This echoes the Pauline commandment, "Pray without ceasing" (1 Thess. 5:17). Through the writings of the Church Fathers and Ascetic Fathers, the Oriental Orthodox are gifted with methods of attaining a life of ceaseless prayer through the continuous recitation of the name of Jesus, the recitation of short prayers or short verses from the psalms. Macarius of Egypt says,

> "There is no need to waste time with words. It is enough to hold out your hands and say, 'Lord, according to your desire and your wisdom, have mercy.' If pressed in the struggle, say, 'Lord, save me!' or say, 'Lord.' He knows what is best for us and will have mercy upon us."[113]

Furthermore, John Chrysostom commends us to

> "constantly call: 'Lord, Jesus Christ, Son of God, have mercy upon me!' in order that this remembrance of the Name of our Lord Jesus should incite you to battle with the enemy. By this remembrance, a soul forcing itself to do this

---

[113] Abba Macarius of Egypt in *Experiences With The Jesus Prayer And Guidelines For Its Practice*, edited by Luis S. R. Vas, (Delhi: ISPCK, 2002), 56.

practice can discover everything which is within."[114]

Through the recitation of short prayers from the Psalms, the Jesus Prayer together with the book of hours, an Orthodox Christian sanctifies time and receives sanctification of life. The Oriental Orthodox communion is blessed with the four widely spread books of hours: the Syriac *Sh'himo*, the Coptic *Agpeya*, the Ethiopian Hours of Abba Giyorgis Saglawi, and the Armenian *Zhamerkootyoon*. Commitment to praying these hours while filling the time between the hours with short prayers like the Jesus Prayer fixes the mind and heart on God and sanctifies our entire being that we may live a life of *martyria* or witness to God.

---

[114] *The Publicans Prayer Book*, (Nashua: Sophia Institute Press: 2000), 564-565.

Chapter 9

Sainthood: Martyrdom, Marriage, and Monasticism

Martyrdom

The Greek word for martyr signifies witness. A witness or a martyr, in the Christian context, is a believer who experienced suffering and persecution unto death for the faith. Christ is said to have "witnessed the good confession before Pontius Pilate." In his footsteps, a vast number of saints have walked to bear witness to their faith. Ignatius of Antioch, a bishop and a martyr of the second century, said on his way to execution,

> "I am writing to all the Churches and I enjoin all, that I am dying willingly for God's sake, if only you do not prevent it. I beg you, do not do me an untimely kindness. Allow me to be eaten by the beasts, which are my way of reaching to God. I am God's wheat, and I am to be ground by the teeth of wild beasts, so that I may become the pure bread of Christ."[115]

Ignatius saw in the offering of his body means to become the bread of Christ. This is an allusion to the Eucharist where Christ's body is offered in the form of bread. Through

---
[115] Ignatius of Antioch, *Epistle to the Romans*, 4.

martyrdom, believers were identifying their tortured bodies with the broken body of Christ. Tertullian speaks of the significance of martyrdom for the Church saying that "the blood of the martyrs is the seed of the Church." The martyrs could not offer their blood without the aid of their discipleship to the Church that shifted their vision from the edge of the sword, fiery furnaces, and hungry beasts to the heavenly kingdom. The Coptic Orthodox Church together with the Ancient Church of Rome offered the largest number of martyrs during the early eras of persecution. In later years, the Church in the East suffered immensely under the yoke of Islamists and Turks.

Many were not strong enough to bear the yoke of persecution in the early Church. Consequently, some fled, others faced persecution and apostatized. Those who fled became the seeds of the monastic movement. Those who remained in the arena but apostatized became a topic of debate for the early Church. Some believed that an apostate is to never be received into communion again until their death. Others, being more lenient, deemed it fit that they be accepted immediately upon repentance. The Church under the guidance of Cyprian of Carthage decided to take a middle path between these two extremes. An apostate would live for the rest of their life in penance and would receive the Eucharist only upon their deathbed.

Monasticism

> "The social and religious climate within which desert spirituality emerged was rooted in the

biblical narrative and reflects how the early Christians, from the time of the apostles, interpreted the gospel message in their lives. Christ asked the disciples to 'follow me.' Desert spirituality is a response to the call to follow Christ."[116]

The end of the persecution marked the beginning of the thriving of monasticism that started in the Church of Alexandria. When many could not offer their blood for Christ's name, they chose to die daily to the passions of the flesh (Rom. 8:36). The early monastic fathers led a simple life outside the city where they could battle their thoughts and seek union with God through prayer. Women often chose to live in monastery like communities that were considered as a home for virgins seeking to consecrate their life to God.

Monasticism came to be a pillar of the Orthodox Church crowned with the virtue of discernment and founded on the three vows of celibacy, renunciation of the world, and obedience. The monastic life was given more order and structure through early founding fathers who developed a variety of styles that cater to different individuals' needs. The Great Abba Anthony of Egypt is considered the founding father of monasticism despite the fact Abba Paul of Thebes was the first to enter the inner eastern desert in Egypt. Abba Paul did not make disciples whereas Abba Anthony made thousands of disciples who imitated his

---

[116] Lois Farag, *Balance of the Heart: Desert Spirituality for Twenty-First-Century Christians,* (Eugene: Wipf and Stock Publishers, 2012), 13.

lifestyle. The account of his life is found in *Vita Antoni*, a writing composed by Athanasius of Alexandria who was a disciple of Anthony and later the great upholder of Nicene orthodoxy. Anthony lived in full solitude for twenty-five years till he reached spiritual maturity. His disciple, Abba Macarius the Great, established monasticism in the western desert of Wadi El-Natroun in Egypt guided by the Cherubim who appeared to him to instruct him in the form of monasticism he was to establish. Abba Amoun was moved through divine revelation to start a monastic community in Nitria that was in communication with the monastic communities of Anthony and Macarius. Abba Pachomius, former pagan, accepted the Christian faith due to the love Christians showed him and chose to become a monk. He established communal monastic communities in Upper Egypt. The Life of Pachomius records him experiencing a vision of an angel with two tablets showing him how he ought to instruct all novices. Prior to the cenobitic life Pachomius established, all monastic communities were isolated and each monk lived separately in a cave. Abba Shenouda the Archimandrite started a large serving monastic community that became a refuge and a haven for many poor and persecuted Christians.

In Greece, Basil the Great took monasticism to Cappadocia where he formed a monastic community. Coptic biographies of Athanasius suggest that he established monastic communities as far as Ireland when he was exiled. John Cassian came from the West and learned monastic wisdom and forms from the East at the hands of Egyptian and Palestinian monks in his *The Conferences* and *The Institutes*. The Syriac Orthodox Church had remarkable ascetics who filled the Church with theological poetry. Examples of such ascetics are Ephraim the Syrian, the harp of the Spirit, and Jacob of Serug, the Flute of the Spirit. The Armenian Apostolic Church had various monastic communities throughout the kingdom of Armenia which were established by Gregory the Illuminator. The Ethiopian Orthodox Church continues to practice monasticism vigorously and ascetically. Ethiopian monks spend lengthy hours in prayers in the heat of the day in small caves carved in the desert that resemble the earliest ascetic tradition of Egypt in every way. Female monastic communities started before Abba Anthony founded monasticism as we are informed that he kept his sister in a convent. Nuns see a great example in the most Holy Theotokos first and foremost as their guide in the ascetic path together with a cloud of saints including Demiana, Amma Sarah, Amma Syncletica of Alexandria, Macrina, and Mary of Egypt.

Marriage

Earlier, I mentioned marriage as a sacrament of the Church by which the eternal union of a man and a woman with God acts as an extension of the union of Christ, the bridegroom, and the Church, the bride of Christ. In this section, I hope to address marriage as a path of salvation. Scripture teaches us that "Marriage is honorable among all, and the bed undefiled" (Hebrews 13:4). Though there is no honor greater than marriage being an extension of the marriage of Christ and the Church, we must remember that another dimension of the honorability of marriage finds its roots in marriage being a path for the salvation of two human beings and their children. The birthing of children is an act of co-creating with God i.e., an act of participating in the process of creation. Motherhood is especially honored as a path of salvation in the words of Paul who says that women "will be saved in childbearing if they continue in faith, love, and holiness, with self-control" (1 Timothy 2:15). There is no doubt that in giving birth mothers choose to suffer for the sake of their children and the continuation of the human race. Christ used this sacrificial act as an analogy for the suffering Church that will be born into the newness of life in the coming age, "A woman, when she is in labor, has sorrow because her hour has come; but as soon as she has given birth to the child, she no longer remembers the anguish, for joy that a human being has been born into the world. Therefore, you now have sorrow; but I will see you again and your heart will rejoice, and your joy no one will take from you" (John 16:21-22). The comforting role of the mother in the house is used by God to shed light on his relationship toward us as the Comforter, "As one whom his mother comforts, So I will comfort you" (Isaiah 66:13). The presence of the woman within her family is an imitation of the work of the Spirit who comforts, nurtures, cares, and gives us His own life.

The role of a husband in his house is no different from the role of a priest in his parish. Husbands must live as spiritual leaders of their home willing to sacrifice their own lives for the salvation of their household. If the bridegroom par excellence has died for His bride, meaning Christ and the Church, then every husband is expected to at least crucify his ego for the sake of the salvation and elevation of his home. A husband ought to be crucified for the comfort of his wife and children. A husband is responsible for leading his relationship with his wife toward God in every way possible.

The Church assists husbands and wives in realizing the objective of their union being attaining saintliness through various advice and regulations. First, the Church insists that her married children have a prayer rule in which they can participate together in building their spirituality. Second, the Church canons advise men and women to abstain from sexual relations during fasts. This is not on account of legalism but is rather a reminder for married couples that the goal of their marriage is the cultivation of a Christian life through which they acquire the Holy Spirit first and foremost. As such, the time used for physical intimacy is transformed during fasting periods into a time of spiritual intimacy. Given the Church's awareness of human weakness and the different levels at which every married couple is, John Chrysostom allowed men and women to engage in sexual relationships even during the fasts if one of them is tempted. He deemed it more fit that they enjoy each other's companionship than they be tormented with lust. Third, the Church requires all her members to become full participants in the life of the Church through the sacramental life of the Church. As such, the rule in the Orthodox Church is for marriage to be only between an Orthodox man and an Orthodox woman. If one spouse is not Orthodox, they are expected to be received into the Church before they receive the sacrament of matrimony. However, some jurisdictions use the principle of economy to allow some leniency in applying this rule on case-by-case basis.

In self-sacrifice, breaking one's ego, raising Orthodox Christian children, and controlling the passions, marriage is not only honorable but is also a martyrdom; a martyrdom which was celebrated on the day of their crowning with the crowns of martyrs.

Epilogue

The Oriental Orthodox Church upheld the Christian Tradition in its fullness as revealed by Christ, handed down by the apostles, and preserved by the Fathers. In the Church, Christ offers the ultimate revelation of the worship of the Trinity with the Church being an icon of the Trinity. We come to the Church for a true living communion with the Holy Trinity. All are called to enjoy the salvation offered to us by God in Christ by the Holy Spirit. In responding to this call, many are martyrs, some are married, some have consecrated their life for Christ in the world, and a few are monastics. Regardless of how one responds, we can live with God worshipping Him in Spirit and in Truth. The Orthodox Church offers the fullness of truth and the fullness of the Spirit without deviation or deficiency.

> In the Church,
> You are invited to become a member of the body of Christ,
> You are invited to live in communion with the Trinity,
> You are invited to live in the communion of saints,
> You are invited to receive salvation, put on Christ, abiding in God and God abiding in you,
> You are invited to receive the grace of adoption, salvation and deification,

You are invited to struggle in your relationship with God and in fighting the passions,

You are invited to be a human being fully alive as God intended you to be,

You are invited to commune with God, experience the Church, and live in the Kingdom of God.

Appendices

The articles in this appendix are not related to the faith but rather serve to provide with a brief history of the Orthodox Church as it thrives in Alexandria, Ethiopia, Eritrea, Armenia, Syria, and India. The first two articles, "The One Catholic and Apostolic Church" and "The Coptic Orthodox Church of Alexandria" are authored by the author of this book. The articles thereafter are translations of excerpts from Fr. Athanasius Al-Makari's book *The Eastern Churches and their Homelands*. If you are already an Orthodox Christian, I truly hope that these articles inform you about the history of your Church in relation to other sister Churches. If you are becoming an Orthodox Christian, I pray that these articles serve you well in learning about the various cultures of Orthodoxy that you may choose what best relates to your own culture.

The One Catholic and Apostolic Church

> *"Stand at the crossroads and look; ask for the ancient paths, ask where the good way is, and walk in it."*
>
> Jeremiah 6:16

The beauty seen in the Orthodox Church is a reflection of its unique long-standing history. The history of the Orthodox Church can be divided into five unique eras that together vividly show the process through which the Church came to be what it is presently.

The Era of the Apostles

This era extends from Christ's ascension, around 33 CE, to the death of John the Beloved, approximately 112 CE. Beginning in Jerusalem, the Church fulfilled Christ's commandment to preach to all nations during this time (Luke 24:47). As the eyewitnesses of Christ's life passed away, the church was able to preserve Jesus' specific oral teachings through the four accounts of the gospel written by Matthew, Mark, Luke, and John. Furthermore, the letters the disciples wrote to strengthen the faith of the new communities they established would later form the majority of the New Testament. The Book of Revelation is the last of the New Testament books written by John of Patmos as a prophecy about the end of days. Paul, the former Christian persecutor and apostle to the Gentiles, wrote fourteen letters (according to Tradition) that make up more than half of the New Testament, while Peter, the former denier of Christ and apostle to the Jews, would write two letters. Together with the rest of the disciples, they carried the Gospel to the end of the world.

The Apostolic Era

In fulfilling Christ's commandments, the apostles made disciples who would carry their apostolic mission after them (Matt. 28:19). The disciples of the apostles are known as the apostolic fathers, who preserved the faith and the earliest traditions given to them by the apostles. Early Christian documents such as the letters attributed to famous figures of this era including Clement of Rome, Ignatius of Antioch, and Polycarp of Smyrna.

The Apologetic Era

The fathers of this era, disciples of the apostolic fathers, devoted their lives to fulfilling the commandment of Peter, "always be ready to give a defense to everyone who asks you a reason for the hope that is in you" (1 Pet. 3:15). They did not cease to defend the faith against the false accusations of non-believers, and confessing the Orthodox faith to the point of bloodshed in the name of Christ. The most notable historical figures would be Irenaeus, Justin Martyr, and Origen, the Dean of the School of Alexandria.

The Patristic Era

The Patristic era is considered to be the most influential era in Orthodox Christian history such that it is known as the golden age. The beauty of this age stems from the writings of our fathers, the councils that reflected the unity of faith, the end of Christian persecution, and the start of monasticism. Despite the beautiful attributes of this era, it was also a period of toil for the Church that has never ceased to carry her Cross with her Bridegroom because of the heresies that surrounded her. Our fathers affirmed the unity of faith and rejected all heresies through the following ecumenical councils:

- The Council of Nicaea (325 CE) against the Arians

- The Council of Constantinople (381 CE) against the Pneumatochians and Apollinarianism
- The Council of Ephesus (431 CE) against the Nestorians

This era began to decline with the council of Chalcedon, which marked the first major schism in Church history in 451 CE. The council was rejected by the Church of Alexandria, Syria, Ethiopia, and Armenia, separating it from the See of Rome, Greece, and Constantinople for theological disagreement on formulating Christology, together with political reasons. Later, such disagreements were mostly resolved with the Eastern Orthodox Church (Greece, Constantinople, and Russia). This happened through dialogues between the sister Churches, mainly during the papacy of His Holiness Pope Shenouda III and the patriarchate of His Beatitude Mar Ignatius Zakka I—may God repose their souls. However, full communion between the Oriental and Eastern families of Orthodoxy has not yet been restored.

This era left the Church with a great quantity of writings and many church fathers to whom the Church can refer to as a reference point. These fathers are divided according to the language they used:

- Greek (Alexandrian and Cappadocian) Fathers: Athanasius of Alexandria, Cyril of Alexandria, John Chrysostom, Basil the Great, and Gregory the Theologian
- Latin Fathers: Jerome and Augustine

- Syrian Fathers: Aphrahat and Ephraim the Syrian

The Post-Schism Era

Beyond the schism in 451 CE, the Church battled against Islamic persecution that came as a result of the Arab invasion of major Oriental Orthodox Sees such as the See of Alexandria and the See of Syria. Orthodox Christians remained strong in Christ and faithful to the Church despite this persecution, guarding the faith committed to their trust (1 Timothy 6:20). During this era, parishioners would use Arabic as the primary language they would practice the faith and celebrate the divine liturgy in Egypt and Syria. This era offered the Church with historians like Ibn El-Asaal, theologians like Gregorios Bar Hebraeus, Bulus Al-Bushi and Gregory Narek and reformers like Pope Cyril IV, the father of reformation. Our churches may be scattered in different areas of the world, but this does not impact our unity because it is the eucharistic unity of our faith that surpasses the limits of time and space. To paraphrase the words of Paul, "there is no longer Copt, Syrian, Ethiopian, Eritrean, or Indian but all are one in the Orthodox Church of Christ."

The Coptic Orthodox Church of Alexandria

The Beginning of the Church of Alexandria

Eusebius of Caesarea affirms the Alexandrian tradition that the Christian faith was brought to Egypt through the preaching of Mark the Apostle and Evangelist. Arriving to Egypt after serving briefly with Paul and Barnabas, Mark searched for a shoemaker to fix his sandals so he can journey through Egypt preaching the Gospel. Mark found a shoemaker named Ananias who agreed to fix his sandals. As Ananias was repairing Mark's sandals, he injured himself and called upon the name of God. Upon hearing this, Mark prayed for Ananias and healed him beginning to teach him about the Christian faith. Ananias and his household would form the center of the Alexandrian Church where liturgies were held and catechizing new believer would begin. After a period of flourishing, pagan mobs stirred masses against Mark and his followers. The mob arrested Mark and began torturing him for three days by tying him to the tail of a horse and making a public example of him across the streets of Alexandria until he reposed in the Lord. Traditional Christians believe Mark to be the son of the man at whose upper room Jesus held the last Supper and the disciples received the Spirit. It is also believed that the same Mark has been the youth who ran away naked when Jesus was being arrested in Gethsemane (Mark 14:51-52).

After his martyrdom, the Church in Alexandria was under the care of Ananias, the first bishop of Alexandria.

Alexandria, as a cosmopolitan Roman province, was destined to hold an esteemed place in the Christian world because of the increasing number of Christians and the numerous resources that Christians could benefit from. The library and pagan school of Alexandria made philosophical literature easily accessible for the rich in society. The Church of Alexandria would eventually have numerous teachers of the faith who would hold classes in their homes for those who desired to become Christian or desired to delve deeper in theological knowledge. These classes would form what would come to be known as the School of Alexandria. While the theological school of Alexandria was in its infancy, Christians often fell victims to Roman persecution, which earned the Coptic Church the epithet of "The Church of the Martyrs."

Martyrdom and Monasticism

The Coptic Church has often been called "The Church of the Martyrs" because of the large numbers of believers who died in the first two centuries after the birth of Christianity in Egypt. Later, Christianity would become the official religion in the Roman Empire and persecution would cease until the Copts refaced persecution under Byzantine policy which aimed to force the Copts to accept the decrees of Chalcedon. Their efforts were met with failure, as Copts continued rejecting it. After the Arab invasion of Egypt, Copts faced many waves of persecution with many being killed or forced to convert against their will. In addition, their churches would be demolished and the stones that once built these churches would be used to build mosques.

During the third and fourth centuries, some fled the persecution and resorted to living in secluded areas in communion with God and away from a troublesome world. This gave rise to the monastic movement which had its roots in Egypt. A rich young man by the name of Anthony heard the Gospel reading in Church saying, "Go sell all that you have and follow Me." He quickly rose, sold what he had, entrusted his sister to a community of virgins and lived outside the village by the river where he learned the basics of monastic life from other ascetics. Eventually, Anthony retreated to the desert until he reached spiritual maturity approximately twenty years later. He had numerous disciples including Athanasius who later became Patriarch of Alexandria. Coptic figures such as Macarius, Pachomious, Shenouda and Amoun would be the pillars of monasticism that monks still learn from and whose wisdom they refer to, to this day.

The School of Alexandria and Theological Controversies

The School of Alexandria produced a large number of Christian theologians who dedicated themselves to the service of the Church. The Patriarchs of Alexandria were often students of the School of Alexandria. This equipped them theologically to engage in the Trinitarian controversies of the third and fourth centuries and the Christological controversies of the fifth and sixth centuries. Origen of

Alexandria is the most famous of the deans of the school of Alexandria because of his numerous works including the *Hexapla*, *On First Principles* and various Commentaries on Scripture. Origen is specially known for his allegorical method of interpreting the Scripture. Origen had a plethora of disciples, whose influence in the Church was unparalleled, such as Gregory the Wonderworker, Gregory Nazianzus, and Basil the Great.

In the fourth century, the Arian, Sabellian, Pneumatomachian, and Apollinarian heresies were circulating across the theological sphere. Athanasius, a disciple of Alexandros, the Patriarch of Alexandria, and Anthony, the father of monks, would emerge as a major figure who combatted such heresies. The Cappadocian fathers: Gregory of Nyssa, Gregory Nazianzus, and Basil the Great, continued the work he began throughout the fourth century. In the fifth century, the Christological controversies produced the figure, Cyril of Alexandria, whose efforts eradicated Nestorianism from the Church, especially in the Council of Ephesus in 431 CE. Twenty years later, Christological controversies would remerge; having been mixed with a complex political matrix in the Council of Chalcedon. The Council marked the schism between the Chalcedonian Churches, now known as the Eastern or Byzantine Orthodox Church, and the non-Chalcedonian Churches, now known as the Oriental Orthodox Churches. The exile of Dioscorus during Chalcedon and the exile of his successor, Timothy II, together with murder of many Copts, left a bitter taste in the mouths of Copts who rejected Chalcedon. This led some to become hopeful that they would possess more religious freedom under the Arab yoke than the Byzantine yoke.

The Coptic Orthodox Church Under Islam

In 640 CE, Arabs under the rule of Amr Ibn Al-As conquered Egypt and the Coptic Church was no longer under Byzantine rule. It was at this time that the Coptic Patriarch was invited back to his rightful position after defeating Cyrus, a Byzantine bishop and governor appointed to subdue Copts and force them to accept Chalcedonianism. However, tolerance toward Copts did not continue very long after the Arab conquest. Admittedly, peaceful times were occasionally part of Coptic history, but they were certainly not the norm. Often Copts were considered second-class citizens, not allowed to possess high military titles, and forced to pay a head tax known as *jizya*. Copts were given three options: pay *jizya*, convert to Islam, or be put to death. Understandably, the theological literature of the Church of Alexandria would decrease after such historical and political developments. However, there were luminous figures that appeared throughout history such as Bulus Al-Bushi, Ibn El-Makin and the sons of Al-Asaal. These figures would leave the Coptic Church with catechetical literature and some discourses on apologetics, mainly defending the Christian faith in the Trinity and the incarnation against Muslim claims. Coptic continued to be the main language of native Egyptians for about three centuries after the conquest. It was not until the ninth century that Arabic would become the main spoken language in Egypt and by the end of the twelfth century that Arabic would be used in Church services.

Shifts in language from Greek to Coptic to Arabic, together with persecution, left the masses with minimal knowledge of their faith. The most the laity knew came from Sunday sermons and the Liturgy. Many clergy were not educated nor worthy. It was common for the rich to pay the Pope to ordain them a priest. Understandably, they would have next to no knowledge of the faith and no interest in shepherding the people.

In the eighteenth and nineteenth century, Roman Catholic and Protestant missionaries visited Egypt with the aim of converting the Copts, but their efforts came to no avail. Pope Cyril IV, known as father of the reformation in the Coptic Church, rejected Italian efforts to bring the Coptic Church under the Pope of Rome. However, Cyril IV enjoyed excellent relations with the Greek Orthodox Patriarch of Alexandria and the Armenian Apostolic Bishop in Egypt. Cyril IV and the Greek Patriarch went as far as entrusting their respective flocks to the other in their absence. Such relationships compelled the Turks to believe that he was attempting to unite the Greeks and Copts. Historians have suggested that this fear is what led to the possible murder of the Coptic Patriarch (considering his premature death) by the Turks with the assistance of the Armenian bishop who likely betrayed Cyril to them. Cyril IV made immense efforts to reform religious and secular education for Egyptians that he built schools where he would teach ordained clergy himself and open a printing press to publish theological books for the benefit of the congregation.

Combatting Protestantism in Egypt was mostly the effort of his successor, Pope Demetrius II, who wrote a letter to his spiritual children in Upper Egypt, admonishing them to place their children in Coptic and public schools rather than Protestant schools and teaching the flock the theological differences between the Orthodox faith and Calvinism.

Habib Guirguis the Archdeacon lived during the papacy of Cyril IV and may have been inspired by his dedication to Christian education. Habib would later take it upon himself to re-establish the theological seminary in Egypt. He dedicated his life to establishing a building for the seminary, taught numerous courses, and formed the Sunday School movement during the papacy of Cyril V. His work in the seminary made him a following of many disciples including priests and bishops, the most famous of whom is the late HH Pope Shenouda III.

The Coptic Orthodox Church Today

The present state of the Coptic Orthodox Church is thanks to the efforts of Archdeacon Habib Guirguis, Cyril VI, Bishop Gregorios of Christian Scientific Research and Education, Fr. Matthew the Poor, HH Pope Shenouda III, and HH Pope Tawadrous II. Pope Cyril VI began his life as Fr. Mina, a monk in the monastery of St. Mary Paramous. Later, he would lead a life of solitude briefly interrupted by serving a parish in Cairo and renewing the buildings of the monastery of St. Samuel the Confessor. He was elected Pope and Patriarch of Alexandria in 1959, which would mark the beginning of a wide-range reformation in the Coptic Orthodox Church. One of the first matters Pope Cyril VI attended to as patriarch was the persisting issues of Ethiopian autocephaly. Following that, Pope Cyril VI reverted his attention to the reformation of Christian education in general with a strong focus on the seminary in Cairo in particular. To this end, Pope Cyril VI ordained Fr. Antonious Al-Suryani (later Pope Shenouda III) as bishop of Christian education and later Bishop Gregorios of Christian Scientific Research and Education. Both would serve the Coptic Church through their sermons and writings. The Coptic Orthodox Church's commitment to the ecumenical movement took place during the papacy of Pope Cyril VI, who often sent Bishop Gregorios to represent the Coptic Orthodox Church, as the latter was the only bishop in the Coptic Church who received a Doctor of Philosophy degree in a field related to theological studies. Bishop Gregorios left the Church with numerous sermons, plethora of writings that have been kept in a thirty-seven-volume encyclopedia, and approximately one thousand pages of his autobiography, recording many events pertaining to Church evolution between the papacy of Pope Cyril and Pope Shenouda. Pope Cyril VI reposed in the Lord in 1971.

Among the disciples of Pope Cyril, was a monastic called Fr. Matta Al-Meskeen or Fr. Matthew the Poor. Matthew (then Youssef Iskander) began his life in a middle-class house and later moved to Alexandria where he received his bachelor's degree in pharmacy. After a successful and wealthy career, Youssef Iskander decided to leave it all behind and become a disciple of Pope Cyril VI (then Fr. Mina the Hermit). Youssef was later tonsured a monk with the name of Fr. Matthew the Poor in the Monastery of St. Samuel the Confessor, which Fr. Mina renewed before his ordination as Pope. From the Monastery of St. Samuel to the Monastery of St. Mary Al-Suryan, Fr. Matthew continued journeying until he settled with twelve monks in the Monastery of St. Macarius where he re-established and rebuilt most of its current buildings. Fr. Matthew had many disciples in the Monastery of St. Mary, the most important of which were Fr. Mousa Al-Paramousi (later Bishop Andrawes of Damietta and Kafr Al-Shikh) and Fr. Antonious Al-Suryani (later Bishop Shenouda of Christian education and eventually Pope Shenouda III). Fr. Matthew left the Church with tens of thousands of pages of theological discourses, biblical commentaries, and monastic wisdom. Fr. Matthew the Poor's books have been translated by his disciples both monastics and laity to many languages which include but are not limited to English, French, and Italian. His famous book *Orthodox Prayer Life* is considered a masterpiece in which he records the writings of the fathers about prayers, whether it be personal or on a liturgical level. Fr. Matthew the Poor is often credited with renewing the monastic life in the Coptic Orthodox Church and is considered by many the father of modern Coptic monasticism. Fr. Matthew the Poor reposed in the Lord on June 8, 2006.

After the departure of Pope Cyril VI, Pope Shenouda III was elected the 117th Pope and Patriarch of Alexandria in 1971 CE. Pope Shenouda continued to teach the congregation as he did since he was elected bishop of Christian education. As bishop and later as Pope, he would dedicate Wednesday nights to give sermons to the congregation, which people often recorded to go back to for spiritual edification. Pope Shenouda's papacy began during the presidency of Anwar Sadat, whose fanaticism made the Church face many trials. Sadat would disapprove of Pope Shenouda's boldness in declaring that Copts are persecuted in Egypt, especially after the murder of 21 Copts in Kosheh village at the hands of a Muslim mob. The conflict between the Pope and the President would conflate to the extent that Pope Shenouda would be placed under house arrest in the Monastery of St. Bishoy in Scetis and would result the imprisonment of several bishops, priests, and Coptic activists. Shortly afterwards, Sadat was murdered by a member of the Muslim brotherhood, approximately a month later. Bishops, priests, and Coptic activists were quickly freed though the Pope continued to remain under house arrest for about five years into the rule of Mubarak, successor of Sadat. After Pope Shenouda's return, he was received warmly by the hierarchs and congregation. The Church grew immensely during his papacy, both in Egypt and in lands of immigration. Pope Shenouda emphasized the role of the Coptic Church in ecumenical dialogue, the World Council of Churches, and the Middle East Council of Churches. During his papacy, the Non-Chalcedonian Orthodox and Chalcedonian Orthodox Churches were able to draft agreed statements, resolving the fifteen-hundred-year old terminological misunderstanding. Pope Shenouda initiated many dialogues with many Christian denominations which he entrusted to Metropolitan Bishoy of Damietta—of Blessed Memory—who was also secretary of the Holy Synod for the majority of Pope Shenouda's papacy. Pope Shenouda reposed in the Lord in March 17, 2012.

Pope Tawadros II is the 118th Pope of Alexandria who succeeded Pope Shenouda to the Patriarchal throne. His efforts in the ecumenical movement have been recognized by the primates of various Churches and denominations including Pope Francis of Rome and Patriarch Kirill of Moscow. Bishop Epiphanius, a disciple of Fr. Matthew the Poor and late abbot of the Monastery of St. Macarius, has often been the representative of the Coptic Orthodox Church in ecumenical meetings and dialogues until the martyrdom of Bishop Epiphanius in 2018. Pope Tawadros has been committed to supporting academic theological endeavors on both an individual and institutional basis. Pope Tawadros continues to outreach his children throughout Egypt and the lands of immigration, spreading the spirit of love throughout the Coptic Church and for this reason he is often given the title "Pope of Love."

The Ethiopian Tawahedo Orthodox Church:[117]

The Beginning of the Ethiopian Church

Rufinus (345-410), a Latin historian who lived in the Mount of Olives in 400 CE, recorded the story of the beginning of the Abyssinian Church as he heard it himself from Edesius, the brother of Frumentius. The latter was ordained first bishop of the Abyssinian Church by Pope Athanasius the Apostolic (328-373) in the year 330 CE in the Cathedral Church of Alexandria. Frumentius was named Abba Salama and returned to Abyssinia to preach the good news of the Gospel allowing the Abyssinia to become the religious capital of Ethiopia. The people of Ethiopia rejoiced in his coming and they called him *Kisati Borhan* meaning "The Revealer of Light." Frumentius established the first Church in Axum and named it after the Theotokos, where he carried to the Ethiopians the liturgy and rites of the Church of Alexandria. Since then, the Ethiopian Church relied completely on the Coptic Church.

Until the papacy of Pope Kyrillos VI (1959-1971), it was customary for the popes of the Coptic Church to ordain an Egyptian bishop for the Church of Ethiopia. In 1959, Pope Kyrillos ordained the first Catholicos Patriarch of Ethiopia granting the Ethiopian Church its autocephaly since then.

---

[117] Athanasius Al-Maqari, *Al-Kana'is Al-Sharqeya w Awtaneha (The Eastern Churches and their Homes)*, (Cairo: Lighthouse Book Center), 2000, 23-52.

Abba Salama, knowing both Greek and Hebrew, translated various religious books to the Ga'ez language, an ancient common Ethiopian language which continues to be the liturgical language of Ethiopia to this day. It is said that Ethiopians have translated the monastic canons of Pachomious, the life of Anthony authored by Athanasius, in addition to a number of patristic books.

Toward the end of the fifth century, around 480 CE, and during the reign of Ameda, the King of Ethiopia, Christianity in Ethiopia witnessed an important revival resulting from the work of a number of missionaries who arrived in Ethiopia. Scholars have disagreed on the identity of those monks. Budge in his book *A History of Ethiopia* suggests that they were a group of Egyptian monks who studied the customs and language of the country and went on to preach the Christian faith, established monasteries and were encouraged to do so by the kings and governors. Other scholars suggest they might have been Syrian. It is unknown whether they were followers of the Chalcedonian Church or the non-Chalcedonian Church.

In the sixth century, the Ethiopian Church brought forth a large number of religious writings in their national language. The country witnessed a revival of the monastic life and monasteries turned into spiritual and intellectual centers that attracted a large number of Ethiopian youth who left the world and struggled in the ascetic life under the guidance of a spiritual elder.

Yemen was under the rule of Ethiopia in the sixth century when king Kaleb Ella Asbeha led an army with the aid of the Byzantine navy on the Himyarite kingdom in 523 CE after the Himyarite king became Jewish and began persecuting Christians. King Asbeha then built numerous Churches throughout Yemen. Yemen was under the rule of Christians since the fourth century although the majority of the population was Jewish. As time passed, Ethiopians managed to expand their territory throughout the Arabian Peninsula until the dawn of the seventh century when the Persian expansion put a limit to Ethiopian rule.

A Historical Era Hidden in Obscurity

Very little is known about the historical events which took place in the Ethiopian Church in the six centuries following the seventh century. After the spread of Islam through the Arabian Peninsula, Amharic Christians began dwelling in the fortified mountains. All communication between Ethiopia and the rest of the world was cut including its ties with Egypt which did not surpass the ordination of an Ethiopian bishop and sending him one after the other.

We know however that Ethiopians suffered persecution in 920 CE due to the government being under Jewish influence and rule. The ties between the Ethiopian Church and the Coptic Church were affected during the papacy of Pope Kozman (920-932 CE) but the Ethiopian Church came back to the embrace of the Coptic Church during the papacy of Pope Theophilus (979-1044 CE). A Christian dynasty was established and continued from 960 to 1268 CE. Often the Church was left without a metropolitan because of the scandals that pagans and Jews would spread in the ears of the governors.

A Religious Revival Beginning in the 13th Century

In 1268 CE, the Ethiopian Church entered a new era of activity and livelihood because of the effort of Abouna Tekla Haymanoot, the abbot of the monastery of "Alebanos" which merged the vigorous life of asceticism with immense energy and hope for the revival of his Church. In the thirteenth century, Yekuno Amlak, a king of a province in Ethiopia since 1270, took advantage of the weakness of the Ethiopian emperors by making an agreement with Tekla Haymanoot entailing that the latter with the Ethiopian Church support Amlak in his demand for the Ethiopian throne. In return, the relations between the Coptic Church and the Ethiopian Church would return, Amlak would grant the Ethiopian Church a third of the Ethiopian lands, and that Tekla Haymanoot would become the leader of Ethiopian monks and be called *Ichege*. Tekla Haymanoot became the mediator between the Egyptian metropolitan and the Ethiopian clergy. All of this came into being and Abouna Salama II, the Coptic Metropolitan of Ethiopia, played a significant role in carrying the religious revival from the Egyptian Church to the Ethiopian Church as he translated a large number of books from Arabic to Ga'ez. This movement continued after his departure and books such as the *Agpeya* [Coptic Book of Hours], the Coptic synaxarion, and the funeral service were translated.

The stability Ethiopia enjoyed since the thirteenth century caused the literary and religious revival to continue. The Church flourished during the reign of Emperor Daoud I (1382 – 1411 CE). The Church reached its peak of revival during the reign of Emperor Zara Jacob (1434 – 1468 CE) who played a major role in the Ethiopian Church as the reviver of her worship, feasts, and hymns. He established new schools and monasteries, combated widespread pagan customs, and ordered religious lessons about the Christian faith be given every Sunday. He also encouraged the carrying over of literary, historical, and religious books from Egypt such as the *Didache*—teachings of the Apostles and *Al-Magmoo' Al-Safawi* by Ibn Al Assal. In addition, he carried over a number of religious festival customs from Egypt to the Ethiopian Church such as the rituals of the feast of Theophany, the feast of Nayrooz,[118] the feast of the Cross and ways of fasting. His revival continued to flourish during the reign of five kings who succeeded him.

In the fourteenth century, internal quarrels emerged between the Ethiopian emperors and the Muslim residents of the country which continued for two centuries. In 1559 CE, Imam Ahmad ibn Ibrahim al-Ghazi nearly destroyed the entire Ethiopian empire and conquered the Ethiopian emperor Galawdewos. He invaded the majority of Ethiopian lands, burned churches, monasteries, religious books, and killed a large number of monks and clergy. This forced many Ethiopians to convert to Islam.

---

[118] Feast of the new ecclesiastical year of the martyrs.

The sixteenth century is considered a low point in the history of Ethiopia as it was at that time, the Ethiopian empire was destroyed. Islam spread throughout the country as Muslims took over most of the countries that overlooked the Red Sea. Ethiopia was likened to an island in the midst of an Islamic Ocean. In this century, Portuguese desire to invade Ethiopia became obvious when they began persuading Ethiopians to become Roman Catholic and to renounce the formulation of the one nature in return for supporting them in their independence. The emperor converted to Roman Catholicism but the Coptic Church eventually returned to its first state in Ethiopia by the middle of the seventeenth century.

In the seventeenth and eighteenth century, a number of violent civil wars began in which most Ethiopian antiquities were destroyed. In the midst of these wars, a new leader came about named Kasa (1818 – 1868 CE) who governed the country in 1855 CE in the name of Emperor Theodore II. During his reign, modern Ethiopia began to emerge as we know it.

It is important to note that Ethiopia is the only country that was not fully conquered by the Arabs in this area. Despite this, Islam spread to a large extent in Ethiopia. It was not until the second half of the 19th century that this began to be reversed through the actions of emperor John IV who forced Muslims to convert to Christianity. Coptic Pope Cyril V (1874 – 1927 CE) condemned him for this action, warned him of the consequences that might befall him for such a course of action, and asked him to stop his methods which were not in conformity with the precepts of God. The emperor obeyed him immediately. When Menelik II (1889 – 1913 CE) became the emperor, he considered Islam the official religion of the Islamic provinces that he made part of his empire and did not interfere in the performance of Islamic rituals carried by the Muslim inhabitants of these provinces. Furthermore, he considered Islamic courts an important part of the legal structure of Ethiopia. This king also established a new capital in the midst of the province Shewa and called it Addis Ababa meaning "the new flower."

His successor Leg Eyassu was sympathetic toward Islam, Turkey, and Germany which raised suspicions among the Ethiopians that the Church excommunicated him. He renounced the governance of Ethiopia in 1916 CE and Zawditu, a daughter of Menelik II was crowned an empress. One of her father's cousins, Ra's Taffari Makounen, competed with her for the government of the country until he was able to conquer Queen Menelik's army. He declared himself an emperor with the name Haile Selassie meaning "Power of the Trinity " which was his baptismal name. The first decade of his reign was a time of turmoil because of his wars with the Italians (1935 – 1936 CE) and for this reason, he was forced to flee the country. Italy invaded Ethiopia until 1941 when the British forces freed Ethiopia from the Italian invasion and Haile Selassie returned to his throne.

The Autocephaly of the Ethiopian Church[119]

When Pope Kyrillos VI was elected Patriarch of Alexandria and before his ordination, he sent to Emperor Haile Selassie and informed him of his election. Pope Kyrillos shared his feelings of love and appreciation in his heart for the Ethiopian nation and Church. He reassured him that Ethiopian demands will be among the first matters he will study and discuss with the Holy Synod after the celebration of his ordination. Despite that gesture, the emperor and the Ethiopian metropolitan refused to accept the invitation or participate in the celebration of the papal ordination. However, Pope Kyrillos kept his promise and sent to the emperor once more until he managed to convince the emperor to send an Ethiopian delegation to Cairo which arrived in June 1959 CE. The head of the delegation declared that he has come to sign an agreement to elevate the Ethiopian Church from a metropolis to a patriarchate and to elevate her metropolitan to a patriarch.

The agreement entailed that the title of the patriarch of Ethiopia would be that of a Catholicos Patriarch, known in Ethiopia as Re'ese Liqane Papasat Echege. The protocol regarding this decree was signed in June 1959 CE and

---

[119] The original subtitle Fr. Athanasius uses is "The stages of the Independence of the Ethiopian Church from the Egyptian Church." In this section, he gives a detailed account of the events leading up to the autocephaly starting from 1876 until 1959 when Ethiopia received its autocephaly. This account is beyond the scope of this book and as such I have omitted the majority of the section and will only relate the account of the autocephaly beginning with the papacy of Pope Kyrillos VI in 1959.

entailed that the Ethiopian Church has been made a national Church. This decree was submitted to the emperor meaning that he must agree for the ordination of a Catholicos Patriarch to take place. The Ethiopian constitution dictated in 1955 CE that the emperor must agree for Ethiopian bishops to be ordained. In this manner, the emperor's desire to control the Church was fulfilled.

Metropolitan Bassilios was ordained a Catholicos Patriarch for the Church of Ethiopia by the hands of Pope Kyrillos and with the participation of Coptic and Ethiopian bishops and metropolitans in the presence of Haile Selassie in the old Cathedral of St. Mark in Cairo. Since this day, the Ethiopian Church became an autocephalous Church. Prior to that date, it was still following the Alexandrian Pope in Egypt.

In September 1974 CE, the communist revolution in Ethiopia began under the guidance of Mengistu Haile Mariam, a leader of the Ethiopia army. The reign of Haile Selassie ended, and he was in exile in Egypt until he died there.

The Ethiopian Church suffered under the yoke of the new governors of the country. The new government did not begin with opposing religion publicly but rather attempted to have the Church support their government. Shortly afterward, they began confiscating Church property.

In February 1976 CE, Patriarch Abune Tewophilos[120] was imprisoned with a number of Ethiopian bishops and metropolitans. Pope Shenouda[121] was asked by an Ethiopian delegation that came to Cairo to ordain a new patriarch in place of the imprisoned patriarch which the government accused of being a wicked man. The Alexandrian Patriarch refused their request as the current patriarch is alive and was not given a chance to defend himself. Pope Shenouda declared that if his mistakes were worthy of excommunication, then so be it. Only then could the patriarchal throne be vacant and a new patriarch would be ordained. He also insisted that the excommunication of a patriarch is a strictly ecclesial matter and a task to be carried out by the Holy Synod and not the government.

The government did not take what the pope said into account and ordained a new patriarch in 1976 CE called Abune Tekla Haymanoot. Consequently, the Coptic Holy Synod declared this ordination uncanonical. In the year after, eight bishops who were ordained during the reign of the emperor were forced to retire…

After the passing away of Patriarch Tekla Haymanoot in 1988 CE, Abune Merkorios was elected to succeed him. The Ethiopian president Mengistu received the new patriarch congratulating him and setting a place for him by his side in official festivals as part of the protocol of the new Ethiopian

---

[120] The Patriarch remained in prison until 1979 and since that date, no trace of him was found.

[121] Successor of Pope Kyrillos VI.

state. However, this was simply a way of hiding the persecutory acts of the government as this communist regime was responsible for:

- The imprisonment and murder of Patriarch Abune Tewophilos
- The imprisonment of metropolitans, bishops, and laity
- The Church forced many to ordain individuals who would submit to the government
- Confiscated Church property
- Spreading atheism among the youth
- Preventing the congregation from praying in Churches
- Banning the use of cars on Sundays
- Cancelling all signs of common Christian festivals which were characteristic of the Ethiopian people
- Changing the Cross square's name and placing large pictures of Lenin[122]

Abune Merkorios resigned for health reasons[123] in July 1992 CE and Abune Paulos was enthroned Patriarch of the Ethiopian Church at a time when the communist dictatorship

---

[122] A Russian revolutionary who interpreted the theories of Marxist communism.

[123] Though Fr. Athanasius writes this in his book, it seems that the reasons for the resignation are disputed. Some suggest that it was in submission to the masses revolting against him. Others suggest he was forced by the government. Together with his supporters, he began a Church in the United States with a synod that came to be known as the synod in exile. This caused a schism that spanned for 27 years which came to an end when both the Synod in Ethiopia and the synod in exile were re-untied in 2018 and Abune Merkorios returned to Ethiopia as patriarch together with Abune Mathias, successor of Abune Paulos, heading the Synod in Ethiopia.

was changing as the government of Mangistu came to an end secondary to being overthrown in 1992 CE. Prior to Abune Paulos's ordination, he was imprisoned for seven years and was exiled to the United States in 1982 CE where he established Churches and centers to serve Ethiopian immigrants. He is considered an old member of the central commission of the World Council of Churches.

The Ethiopian Church Today[124]

Pastorally, the Church of Ethiopia is divided into sixteen eparchies or dioceses including that of Addis Ababa and dioceses outside Ethiopia including Jerusalem, Sudan, Western Europe, Kenya and Djibouti. The number of members of the Ethiopian believers exceeds 30 million out of a total of 53 million Ethiopians.[125] They are shepherded by a large number of clergy; distributed into twenty thousand parishes throughout Ethiopia and 5536 traditional schools throughout the various eparchies. Priests of the various Ethiopian churches enroll in these schools. There are six schools that are specialized in the training of priests. Since the beginning of 1985 CE, there are four thousand Sunday schools which have been arranged according to the teachings of the Ethiopian Church.

In Addis Ababa, the college of the Holy Trinity, a theological school, was established by Emperor Haile

---

[124] The original title in Fr. Athanasius Al-Maqari's book is "The Internal Structure of the Church of Ethiopia"

[125] This statistic goes back to the early 1990s.

Selassie with the efforts of Fr. Morcos Dawood when he served in Ethiopia.[126] There is also the theological school of St. Paul west of Addis Ababa to prepare priests for higher ecclesial responsibilities. This college has a section for biblical studies and is filled with students who are priests, monks, and deacons.

---

[126] Fr. Morcos Dawod is credited with translating the Ethiopian Liturgies to Arabic and English.

The Eritrean Tawahedo Orthodox Church[127]

It was customary to consider Eritrea as part of the Ethiopian diocese or patriarchate while the people of Eritrea considered themselves as headed by the Coptic Patriarchate. The spiritual care giver for this area used to be the abbot of the monastery of Debre Bizen whose role was similar to that of the Ichege in Ethiopia. This monastery is considered the greatest and most famous in Eritrea. It is located on the mountain tops of Bizen and dates back to 1350 CE.

The Autocephaly of the Eritrean Church[128]

In October 1990 CE, Pope Shenouda III chose two of the Eritrean monks who graduated the Coptic Orthodox theological seminary in Cairo and ordained them general bishops in the Coptic Church.

In March 1994 CE, after a period of cohort theological education in Cairo, five abbots of monasteries in Eritrea were chosen to be ordained as bishops in the Church of Eritrea. Bishop Macarius, an Eritrean bishop, translated the

---

[127] Athanasius Al-Maqari, *Al-Kana'is Al-Sharqeya w Awtaneha* (*The Eastern Churches and their Homes*), (Cairo: Lighthouse Book Center 2000), 85-89.

[128] Fr. Athanasius Al-Makari includes details of the events leading up to the autocephaly of the Eritrean Church starting in 1896 CE until 1990 CE when Eritrea received its autocephaly. This account is beyond the scope of this book and as such I have omitted the majority of the section and will only relate the account of the autocephaly beginning in 1990 CE during the papacy of Pope Shenouda III.

Arabic curriculum the five bishops were to study from to Tigrinya, the language of Eritrea. In May 1994 CE, they were commissioned to shepherd the Church in Eritrea and act as a nucleus for a future Eritrean Holy Synod as per the request of the Church and the State there.

On the day of Pentecost of June 1994 CE, the Holy Synod of the Eritrean Orthodox Church was established following the ordination of five bishops by Pope Shenouda and the attendance of sixty Coptic Orthodox metropolitans and bishops. The prayers of ordination were recited in Arabic, Coptic, English, French, and Tigrinya in the presence of a chorus from the Eritrean Church which participated with hymns from the Eritrean Church on this glorious day.

On May 8, 1998 CE (Feast of St. Mark), the first patriarch of the Eritrean Orthodox Church was crowned with the name of "His Holiness Patriarch Philoppos I" by the hands of Pope Shenouda. Eritreans call him with their preferred title "Abune Philoppos I" which is the title by which he was called during the Liturgical prayers of his ordination. When he received the staff, the following prayer was recited, "Receive the shepherd's staff from the hand of our father the Patriarch Abba Shenouda that you may shepherd the flock of God which you have been entrusted with and whose blood will be required at your hand." And since this day, the Eritrean Orthodox Church has become an autocephalous Church.

A protocol between the Coptic and Eritrean Churches was signed by both Patriarchs. It contained fifteen articles; the most important of which are:

- The name of the Patriarch of Alexandria and the Patriarch of Eritrea is to be recited in all liturgies
- The decrees of both Holy Synods are to be exchanged on a regular basis
- A Holy Synod meeting for the two Churches is to be held every three years or whenever necessary
- In the ecumenical dialogue meetings discussing dogmatic differences with other denominations beyond the Oriental Orthodox family, the two Churches will send one general delegation.

On May 29, 1998 CE, The Alexandrian Pope visited Eritrea with Patriarch Philoppos I and the delegates accompanying him to enthrone the new patriarch on his throne in Asmara. Members of political and religious circles headed by the Eritrean President Isaias Afwerki joyfully received and welcomed the two patriarchs.

The Eritrean Church Today

Now Eritrea encompasses 1500 Churches with Asmara, the capital of Eritrea, having 22 Churches. The Church has 22 monasteries and three convents attached to the monasteries.

The Syriac Orthodox Church of Antioch[129]

Christianity's Arrival to Syria

The Christian faith has been in Syria since the dawn of Christianity and continued to grow until it became widespread.

Monasticism came to Syria through Egypt and with it came asceticism and ceaseless worship in the land. The number of monasteries increased together with the number of ascetics since the fourth century. The most famous of such monks is Simeon the Stylite who reposed in the Lord in 459 CE. His relics were buried in the Church of Constantine in Antioch.

After the Council of Chalcedon in 451 CE, the Church of Antioch quickly deteriorated due to the persecution that befell it from the Byzantine Church and Byzantine emperors. The Church of Antioch barely survived and would have further deteriorated had it not been for the emergence of the Antiochan bishop and saint Jacob Baradeus (500-578 CE). Jacob Baradeus migrated through the lands of Syria until he arrived in Egypt to console, strengthen, and organize the Churches that had been dispersed because of the persecution. He ordained new shepherds and bishops to replace the ones whose dioceses were left empty due to their arrest in their

---

[129] Athanasius Al-Maqari, *Al-Kana'is Al-Sharqeya w Awtaneha* (*The Eastern Churches and their Homes*), (Cairo: Lighthouse Book Center 2000), 98-109.

thirty-five-year struggle against the Byzantine empire. If it were not for him, the Byzantine Church would have brought the Churches of Egypt and Syria to an end.

The Persians conquered Syria in 540 CE forcing Justinian, the Byzantine emperor, to sign a peace treaty with them entailing that he would pay them a tribute. When Heraclius became emperor in 610 CE and began a new Byzantine dynasty, the Persians expanded until they almost reached Constantinople. Persians continued to wage war on Syria every year to expand their territory until they established their dominion over Antioch, Damascus and eventually Jerusalem in 615 CE. The Persians also took away the holy wood of the Cross to their capital. This caused Heraclius to wage war against them, having had the Church's treasury under his command by the Patriarch of Constantinople. Heraclius was successful in his quest, especially in Nineveh, until he managed to have them retreat to the doors of their capital in 628 CE having also brought back the holy Cross.

The History of Antioch:
The Religious Capital of Syria

Antioch held an esteemed place in the early Christian era having been the mother Church for Gentile Christians. As such, it received a second place as a center of the newly established Christian faith after Jerusalem, having had the disciples (meaning the believers in Christ) be called Christians there for the first time (Acts 11:26). Some believe that the Greek pagans of Antioch were the ones who called the followers of the new religion, "Christians." The synod which gathered in Jerusalem decreed to absolve Christian gentiles from the yoke of the Jewish law as this issue was pressing in Antioch (Acts 15). The Antiochian Christian community supported Paul in his movement against the Judaizers, those who insisted on a return to Jewish customs.

From Antioch, Paul started his three missionary journeys (Acts 13:1, 15:36, 18:32) as he returned there twice after his first two journeys offering an account of each journey to the Church of Antioch (Acts 14:26, 18:22). According to tradition, the first bishop of Antioch is Peter the Apostle. With the dawn of the second century, the Church of Antioch was well organized due to the efforts of Bishop Ignatius of Antioch who composed seven epistles while journeying from Antioch to Rome, where he was ultimately martyred. Through these letters, the Church was able to understand the clear distinction between the role and significance of bishops, presbyters, and deacons in the Church of God. By the fourth century, the city of Antioch reached its peak of flourishing that Julian the Apostate (361-363) said of it, "It is a joyful, pleasure-loving, and populous city."

The residence of the See of Antioch was in Antioch until 518 CE when it was moved to the monasteries between the rivers due to the oppression and persecution the Church suffered then. The Syrians were able to expand toward Iraq where the borders between the Byzantine and Persian empires ceased to exist eastward of Euphrates.

The deterioration of the city was due to three major factors:

- The first factor: the numerous earthquakes which destroyed most of its major buildings. The first major earthquake lasted three days and occurred in 115 CE during the reign of Emperor Trajan, who managed to escape death during the earthquake. Between 455 and 458 CE, another earthquake came upon the city destroying a major part of it, followed by another earthquake that occurred ten years later. In May 526 CE, a fearsome earthquake took place which destroyed many buildings including the Church which Constantine built. This earthquake caused the death of the Byzantine Patriarch Ephrasius, among thousands of other people. John of Nikiu, the Coptic Church historian, attributed this earthquake to the wrath of God resulting from the exile of Severus of Antioch from his see. When Justinian I became emperor, he dedicated a lot of efforts toward rebuilding Antioch and its Churches. Unfortunately, however, two earthquakes hit the city in 528 CE and 539 CE causing the city major losses. Historians relate that the first of these earthquakes occurred on Wednesday November 29th for an entire hour starting at 3 PM, during which the walls of the city fell, and four thousand individuals died. In 581 CE, another earthquake affected city buildings followed by another earthquake in 589 CE causing the Cathedral of the city to fall.

- The Second factor: the Persian conquest in 531 CE which brought the glory of the city to an end.
- The third factor: the Arab conquest in 638 CE which brought a final separation for the city from the rest of the Christian world.

The Great Schism (1054 CE) and the sad events that followed it included the exile of the Antiochian Patriarch to Constantinople in 1100 CE. The residence of the Antiochian See was moved to Mor Hananyo Monastery near Mardin, Turkey in 1166 CE during the patriarchate of Michael the Great. However, he did not use the monastery as his residence neither did his successors. Rather, they chose to reside in the areas surrounding Sis and Malatya until Patriarch Ignatius Bin Wahib who resided in the Monastery of Mor Hananyo, rendering it the official Patriarchal residence since the thirteenth century.

In the modern era, the city has been conquered twice: first, during the reign of Mohammed Ali in 1840 CE, and second, during World War I, as the city became a French colony. The city was later returned to the Turkish Republic.

Today, nothing remains of Antioch's fame for the Syriac Church but its memory and historical legacy. The Church of Antioch, which was once one Church, now encompasses numerous denominations beside the mother Orthodox Church (i.e., the Syriac Orthodox Church) such as the Greek Patriarchate of Antioch, the Maronite Patriarchate, the Syriac Catholics, the Greek-Catholics, the Assyrians, the Patriarchate of Armenia, and the Patriarchate of Georgia.

However, none of these denominations have their main patriarchal residence in Antioch.

The Antiochian Patriarchate, prior to the aforementioned divisions, used to extend from Taurus and Cilicia in the North to Lebanon and the borders of Palestine in the south, and from the Persians lands in the East to the Mediterranean Sea in the West. Despite Greek being the main language of the government and the major cities and Syriac being the main language in public circles, distant areas, and mountains, they all were led by one ecclesial hierarch without partiality.

When Nestorius of Constantinople was exiled from his see because of his heterodox teachings, the Antiochian Patriarchate faced a lot of turmoil because of Nestorius's allies causing them to separate from the Patriarchate and forming what is now known as the Assyrian Church. The Assyrian Church began its missionary activity since then to the Arabian Peninsula where Bahira[130] the monk was a major figure prior to the appearance of Islam. Their missionary activity then spread to the East where they established a Church in India now known as the Chaldean Syrian Church. The Syriac Orthodox Church of Antioch eventually formed ties with India forming the Syriac Orthodox Church of India or the Malankara Jacobite Syrian Orthodox Church.

The Patriarchal residence of the Syriac Orthodox Church has been well established in Damascus since 1959

---

[130] Historians believe Bahira to have been a major influence on Muhammed, the prophet of Islam, and his message.

CE. The title of the Patriarch of the Syriac Orthodox Church is "His Holiness Mor Ignatius (name), Patriarch of Antioch and all the East, and the Supreme Head of the Syriac Orthodox Catholic Church." His religious rights include the ordination of the Catholicos of the Syriac Orthodox Church of India, metropolitans, and bishops, the convening of synods and councils, and the consecration of the *Myroon* [i.e., Chrismation Oil].

The Arab Conquest

The Syrians, who rejected the Council of Chalcedon, were fed up with the persecution and heavy taxes imposed on them by the Byzantine empire to the extent that Syrians did not contest or complain about the Arab conquest. The era between 633 and 636 CE marked the rule of Umar Bin El-Khatab, who managed to cast the Byzantines out of Syria with many citizens converting to Islam.

When Arabs conquered Damascus under the guidance of Abi Ubaidah in the battle of Yarmouk in 635 CE, they guaranteed the Christians could keep fifteen churches and freedom of worship. The Umayyad Caliphate made Damascus the capital of their large empire which spread over the course of the eighth and ninth centuries. Thus, Damascus became one of the most important Islamic cities upon the rule of the Umayyads between 661 and 750 CE. The Umayyad Mosque is considered one of the most significant Muslim monuments in Damascus. This mosque was formerly a Church established by Emperor Theodosius I around 375 CE and was later converted to be a mosque.

Syria became a mere Abbasid province and thus its great status, which it held for nearly a century before the fall of the Umayyads, began to deteriorate. The Abbasids made Baghdad the capital of their empire. Their rule began to weaken around the end of the 9th century after their rulers and leaders were chosen from among the Turks. Thus, a number of independent emirates and kingdoms were formed; the most famous of such are the Tulunids who governed Syria and Egypt between 878 and 905 CE, the Hamadins in Aleppo between 944 and 1003 CE, and the Egyptian Fatimids who governed Southern Syria while the North fell under the rule of the Seljuk and Turkish princes.

The Crusaders conquered Syria around the end of the eleventh century but were again cast out a century later by the efforts of Saladin, the Ayyubid. Immediately after the end of the Latin rule in Jerusalem, which came as a result of the crusades, Antioch fell under the Egyptian Mamluks by the end of the thirteenth century. One of the negative effects of the crusades has been the annihilation of the Eastern theological schools putting an end to the glorious age of Syriac literature.

The Mongol and Ottoman Conquests

Syria fell victim to the wars of the Mongols, whose rule came to an end after they were conquered by Saif ad-Din Qutuz, a Mamluk prince, in the battle of Ain Jalut in 1260 CE. Syria was later conquered by the armies of Timur, a Mongol who committed crimes of murder and plundering, destroyed Damascus, and burned mosques and schools. The

Mongol conquest of Syria was the most difficult time the Syriac Church had to endure as Christians used to flee to the mountains to escape being slaughtered like sheep. When waves of persecution would calm, they would come off the mountains to see their houses, churches, and monasteries desolate. In 1516 CE, Sultan Salim I conquered Syria establishing the Turkish Ottoman rule causing further weakening of Syria.

The Syriac Orthodox Church Today

The number of the children of the Syriac Church has decreased. Most of them reside now in Syria, Lebanon, Iraq, Jordan, Turkey, Egypt, Europe, North America, South America and Australia. Together with Syriac Church in India–which had historical ties with Syriac Orthodox Church– they form two million people, the majority of which reside in India.

The Malankara-Syriac Orthodox Church of India[131]

The Formation of the Malabar Church

Malabar is a province in the southwest of India known as the province of Kerala. In this area, a Christian community was formed creating the Malabar Church. According to their tradition, Thomas the Apostle preached in India in 52 CE and continued to preach there for twenty years until his martyrdom at the hands of soldiers near Madras. His tomb remains there to this day and is characterized by a cross on top of it that dates to the seventh century. The Malabar Church holds two feasts for Thomas: from December 18th-21st in commemoration of his torture and martyrdom, and July 3rd which marks finding his relics in the 4th century. Their tradition holds that he ordained for them a number of deacons and priests from four Indian families.

We have no historical evidence that proves the existence of Christianity in India before 550 CE. It is difficult to state the story of Indian Christianity in its first five centuries because of the Synod of Diamper, which was held in 1599 CE in which Meneses, an Archbishop of Goa from Portuguese origins, decreed to destroy all ancient documents. Despite that, we have information through the

---

[131] Athanasius Al-Maqari, *Al-Kana'is Al-Sharqeya w Awtaneha* (*The Eastern Churches and their Homes*), (Cairo: Lighthouse Book Center 2000), 166-174.

writings of other historians and pilgrims such as Pantaenus of Alexandria (2nd century). The first ecumenical council indicates the presence of a bishop by the name of John and the title of Bishop of all Persia and India.

The Assyrian Church of the East had a major role in the formation and shepherding of the Malabar Church until the 16th century. An ancient Assyrian author called Yomiat Sert indicates that Daoud the bishop of Arabs decided to leave his See and dedicate himself to evangelize in Indian lands. The persecution which Shapur II (309-379 CE) launched against the Assyrian Christians in Persia dispersed many of them until they sought refuge in Southern India.

The local tradition of the Church of India claims that Middle Eastern and Persian groups have migrated to India. In 345 CE, Middle Eastern Christians came to the Malabar province under the leadership of a Christian merchant from Jerusalem called Thomas Kana. Those who came with him form a group known as "The Southerners" which are distinct from the Christians who received the faith from Thomas the Apostles who are known as the "The Northerners."

In the eighth and ninth centuries, there were two major waves of immigration of the Assyrians to India accompanied by Persian bishops. The first was under the leadership of Bishop Thomas and a number of his followers in 774 CE and the second was under the guidance of Mor Sabor. India granted these two groups a lot of rights and privileges, keeping only the application of criminal law as a responsibility of the government and leaving the governance in other matters to these two groups. The Assyrians began preaching the Christian faith among the Indians, built churches and erected crosses in the major squares, some of which remain to this day. The Malabar Church continues to flourish in India while it used the Syriac language and the Eastern Syriac rite in its liturgical worship.

Catholicos Saliba Zakka (714-728 CE) granted the Church of India its autocephaly granting its bishop the title 'Metropolitan.' The Church of India, however, continued to follow the Chaldean Catholicos as Ishoyahb III (650-666 CE), who preceded Saliba Zakka, and Timothy I (870-823 CE), who succeeded Saliba Zakka, insisted that the Church of India will always remain under their rule.

In the twelfth century, Granganor became the residence of the Indian bishop Mor Youhanna. By the beginning of the 14th century, Mor Yacoub was called Metropolitan of all India. In 1490 and 1503 CE, the Chaldean Catholicos sent two groups of bishops to the Malabar Church. The second group reported back to the Catholicos in 1504 CE informing him of the Portuguese presence throughout the land.

The Portuguese Occupation and the Latinization of the Indian Church

In 1549 CE, Portugal conquered India and had it under its rule. The Portuguese aimed to expand their religious and political rule through having the Christians of India under their protection. The presence of Eastern Assyrian bishops came as an obstacle in the way of such protection. To this end, the Portuguese stopped any Eastern Assyrian bishop from entering India after the passing away of Metropolitan Mor Yacoub in 1552 CE. Mor Youssef Sulaqa was sent to the Malabar Church by Patriarch Shem'on VII Isho'yahb in 1556 CE and was kept with the Portuguese for eighteen months before he could enter India. The last Assyrian bishop to enter the Malabar Church was Mor Abraham in 1597 CE.

A sad era of the Malabar Church begins with the Jesuit missionaries that came from Rome in 1598 CE as they were able to enter India after the Portuguese occupation. In 1599 CE, the synod of Diamper forced Latin canons and customs on the Christians of India. They were to submit to the first Jesuit bishop appointed for them by Rome, Francis Ros, who was under the Archbishop of Goa, Aleixo de Menezes.

Rome used inquisitors in India against anyone who opposed the Catholic Church with the aim of eradicating Eastern Christianity from India. The greatest crime they committed against history and civilization was the burning of all books and ancient documents that would resemble any trace of Nestorianism. The Church there had nothing left of its Eastern rite but the use of the Syriac language in the celebration of the Liturgy.

The Malabar Church follows the Syriac Orthodox Church of Antioch

Due to the increasing resentment against Rome, the Indian Church began sending ambassadors to the bishops overseeing Eastern Churches with the hope of consecrating a bishop. It seems that the archdeacon attempted to contact the Chaldean Patriarch with the hope of consecrating a bishop for them. In 1652 CE, a letter from a man named Mor Eithalaha claimed that the Pope of Rome consecrated him a Metropolitan over the Christians of India. The Portuguese, however, captured this man and kept him in the Jesuit center in Mylapore. After a series of sad events, news spread that Mor Eithalaha drowned to death. This angered the Christians of India and caused them to group themselves under the leadership of the archdeacon of the Church. Because ordaining the archdeacon was not an option in the absence of bishops, twelve presbyters laid their hands on him in 1653 CE declaring him a bishop with the name Thoma I. Knowing that his ordination was not canonical, he contacted Rome but his conditions were denied together with his ordination. Thoma I then turned to the Patriarch of Antioch who sent Mor Gregorious the Metropolitan of Jerusalem to India in 1665 CE. It is unclear whether Thoma I received a canonical ordination from Mor Gregorious or not. The teachings of the Syriac Orthodox Church of Antioch would begin spreading in India forming the Malankara Orthodox Syrian Church.

The Malankara Church in India returned to use the Syriac rites and abandoned much of the Latin customs that permeated it. The Church in India came to know the rite of the West Syriac Church of Antioch, and the rites of the sacraments, etc. This compels us to believe that Mor Gregorious the Metropolitan of Jerusalem canonically ordained Mor Thoma I.[132]

---

[132] The article explores the impact of Protestant missionaries on the Malankara Orthodox Syrian Church and the various factions that began

The Malankara Church in Modern Times

In 1912 CE, Patriarch Abdelmessih declared that the Indian Patriarchate is affiliated with the Syriac Orthodox Church and functions in communion with the Syriac Orthodox Church although it is autocephalous when it comes to administrative matters. In September 1982 CE, the Malankara Orthodox Church of Mor Thoma celebrated its 70th year anniversary of the declaration of its autocephaly in Kerala.

In August 1993 CE, the Syriac Orthodox Patriarch of Antioch ordained a Metropolitan to shepherd the Syriac Church in North America for the Syriac Indians who follow the Malankara Orthodox Syrian Church that is headed by a Catholicos Patriarch. The New Metropolitan celebrated the Liturgy in Malayalam in the presence of Syriac Christians from Damascus, America, and India.

In November 1996 CE, Metropolitan Paulos Mor Gregorios reposed in the Lord at age 74. Mor Gregorios is considered a prolific theologian of the Malankara Orthodox Syrian Church and one of the leaders of the Ecumenical movement. Mor Gregorios worked as an advisor to the Ethiopian emperor Haile Selassie I and was the president of the international conference organized by the World Council of Churches in America in 1979 CE. He was elected a president of the Council of Churches in 1983 CE until 1991 CE. He was the dean of the theological seminary in Kottayam and assisted in the Orthodox center in Delhi. He

---

to emerge. This part has been omitted in translation as it mainly introduces the reader to the other Christian denominations in India which is beyond the scope of this book.

was described by Konrad Raiser, secretary of the World Council of Churches, as a major theologian and thinker of this generation. He has left his mark on the Church and the generations of priests in the ages to come.

The Malankara Church Today

The number of Orthodox Christians in India now exceeds 1.5 million according to the statistics of the 1980s. The Church has twenty dioceses, fifteen metropolitans, five bishops, and a seminary that was established in 1815 CE. The seminary in Kottayam currently offers academic degrees including doctoral degrees. The Church possesses an evangelization center and an Orthodox center for education in Delhi. Mor Gregorios, who reposed in 1902 CE, is considered the most influential figure in the Orthodox Church after Thomas the Apostle. The Youth movement was established in 1908 CE and the Church produces tens of magazines for educational purposes.

Approximately one thousand parishes, eight hundred priests and one and half million believers followed the Patriarch of the Malankara Church until 1983. This is in addition to the believers in Kuala Lumpur, Singapore, Bahrain, Dubai and other countries where Indians work outside India.[133]

---

[133] The Orthodox Church in India suffers from occasional waves of violence among local Orthodox Christians as there is a group that is in communion with the Syriac Orthodox Church of Antioch and a group that impeached communion with the Syriac Patriarch of Antioch. We hope and pray that the two groups would return to communion and that the schism ceases to exist.

The Armenian Apostolic Church[134]

The Beginning of the Armenian Church

Church tradition informs us that the two apostles Thaddeus and Bartholomew preached the Christian faith to the Armenians in the middle of the first century. The Armenian Church upholds this tradition as it proves its apostolicity. However, there is no historical evidence for such claim. What is attested by historical claims is that by the end of the second century, there was a large community in southern Armenia who were preached to by the Syrians who came from Edessa, who King Abgar IX became Christian.

The Armenian historian Faustus Bizans, who lived in the fourth century, mentions that the first groups that became Christian were the Jews who lived there. In the third century, historical documents mention the presence of an Armenian bishop named Mirogen in Eastern Cappadocia. Armenians would eventually cut themselves from the Persians and be more inclined to form ties with the Roman Empire. This made them vulnerable to the attacks and persecutions of the Zoroastrians.

The country received the faith at the hands of Gregory the illuminator who is known as Gregory the Armenian (301 – 325 CE) when the saint baptized Tiridates III. As such,

---

[134] Athanasius Al-Maqari, *Al-Kana'is Al-Sharqeya w Awtaneha* (*The Eastern Churches and their Homes*), (Cairo: Lighthouse Book Center), 2000, 193-204.

Armenia is the first state that made Christianity its official religion in 301 CE. Leontius, the Metropolitan of Caesarea in Cappadocia, ordained Gregory the illuminator bishop of Armenia.

The rank of Armenian Catholicos[135] was hereditary within one family. The Metropolitan of Caesarea in Cappadocia was responsible for the ordination of the archbishop of Armenia. In 374 CE, Armenians rejected their dependence on the Church of Caesarea during the reign of Papas who ended the life of the reforming Patriarch Nerses by poisoning him. Wanting to ordain a patriarch that he would desire and knowing that the bishop of Caesarea might not accept that, he decreed that the new patriarch be ordained by Armenian bishops in his country. This continued to be their custom of ordaining the Armenian patriarch since that day.

Gregory established a diocese in Etchmadzin, meaning the descent of the Son of God, near the mount of Ararat. The Cathedral of Etchmadzin was built in 303 CE and is considered one of the most ancient cathedrals in the world. It was renovated in 1977 CE in the time of Catholicos Faskin I. The celebration of its consecration was attended by Poemen, Patriarch of Russia, and Matthew, Patriarch of the Church of Thomas in Malabar in India among other church hierarchy. The celebration was attended by 40000

---

[135] The Catholicos is the title of the head of the Armenian Church. The rank of Patriarch comes under that of the Catholicos; however, the patriarch acts independently of the Catholicos.

Armenians from the 6 million members of the Armenian Church worldwide.[136]

The historical birth of Christianity in Armenia took place around Lake Van, east of Greek Cappadocia and north of Syrian Osrhoene and Adiabene. Christian influence came from both of these directions from the third to the fifth century.

Although Gregory the Armenian was married, following his ordination, he left his home and freed himself for his apostolic role as bishop. After heading the Armenian Church for 25 years, his son, Aristakis (325-333 CE), succeeded him and attended the first ecumenical council of Nicaea. His older and married brother Frtanis (333-341 CE) succeeded him. After his departure, his son Hosik (341-347 CE) succeeded him. This hereditary element in Church hierarchy is part of the Armenian identity which was inherited from the priestly custom of the Old Testament.

Nerses the Great (353-373 CE) is recognized for his organization of the Armenian Church after the departure of Catholicos Gregory and his successors. After his ordination to the bishopric at the hand of the Cappadocian bishop in 364 CE, he returned to Armenia, organized Church canons and monastic canons, organized life in monasteries, and established hospitals and orphanages. The author of his biography writes, "At the time of Nerses, you could not find a single beggar throughout Armenia."

---

[136] This statistic was retrieved in the end of the 1990s.

The Armenian Church did not participate in the second ecumenical council (381 CE) but it adopted all its teachings and decrees.

Since the beginning of the fifth century, the saintly monk Mesrob (440 CE) managed to develop the Armenian alphabet[137] in 406 CE. It mainly depended on the Greek and Pahlavi alphabets to protect the independence of his Church and its identity. He began, with two of his disciples in Samosata, to translate the book of Proverbs and the New Testament from Greek. Prior to that, the Armenian Church relied in its readings and liturgies on the Greek tradition in the western parts and the Syriac tradition in the eastern parts. Most of the congregation knew neither language which deemed it necessary that the prayers and readings of the Church be translated to the language of the congregation. This project was adopted by Catholicos Isaac the Great or Hasak the Great (390-440 CE) and the project came to completion and was published in 411 CE.

The king Vramshapuh was eager to generalize this translation throughout Armenian regions. The Catholicos began organizing the Armenian Church and develop its theological education. Mesrob and his companions finished translating the Holy Bible to Ancient Armenian in 436 CE.

---

[137] The Armenian Alphabet consists of 36 letters and is written from left to right. It is comparable to Latin in its grammar and verb tenses. It is a rich and tractable language that gives room to the formulation of terms necessary to express scientific, theological, and philosophical ideas. It continued to be used until the 19th century until it was overruled with a new common tongue. However, it is still used as the Liturgical language to this day.

Another group of translators emerged and began translating the liturgy from Syriac to Armenian, together with a number of philosophical and patristic writings. This era marked the peak of literary development. It is worth noting that the original of some of these translated texts have been lost and are only found in their Armenian translation, such as excerpts of the writings of Ephraim the Syrian (306-373 CE), Irenaeus (130-200 CE), and Plato the philosopher.

The Armenian Church did not participate in the third ecumenical council, which took place in Ephesus in 431 CE, though it accepted its teachings and canons. Due to the wars Armenia went through and the chaotic political matrix of the country, the Armenian Church did not participate in the Chalcedonian controversy regarding Christology. The Armenian Church did not attend the Council of Chalcedon in 451 CE and fifty years later, the Armenians rejected this council despite Byzantine pressure to accept it. In a council called Dvin I in 506 CE, the Armenian Church condemned the Council of Chalcedon. In 551 CE, the council of Dvin II was convened and it embraced Miaphysitism in which the Armenian Church together with her Oriental Orthodox sister churches acknowledge the one incarnate nature of God the Word.[138]

---

[138] The Local Councils of Armenia:
  -Dvin I (506 CE): condemned the Council of Chalcedon
  -Dvin II (551 CE): embraced Miaphysitism and composed Armenian history
  -Dvin III (608 CE): caused the separation between Armenian and Georgian churches

Transitions of Armenian Patriarchal Residence

In the eighties of the fifth century, the patriarchal residence was moved from Etchmiadzin to Dvin where the council of 554 CE was convened to affirm the Armenian rejection of Chalcedon which ended communion with the Byzantine Church. In 928, the patriarchal residence was then moved by Lake Van in a city called Aktamar, a city built between 915 and 921 CE that is considered an architectural work of art. Catholicos Sarkis I moved the patriarchal residence to Ani in 992 CE. The patriarchal residence then moved between the following regions: Cilicia, Dzovk, Hromgla, and finally in Sis. After the fall of the Cilician kingdom, Armenian bishops demanded the return of the patriarchal residence to its earlier location in Etchmiadzin in 1441 CE. This was met with resistance on the end of Cilician

---

- Carana (643 CE): attempted to reconcile the Armenian and Byzantine churches
- Dvin IV (649 CE): attempted to reconcile the Armenian and Byzantine churches
- Dvin V (718 CE): condemned the Armenian Pauline heresy
- Manzikert (726 CE): united the dogmas of the Armenian and Syriac churches
- Shirak (826 CE): attempted to reconcile the Armenian and Byzantine churches
- The Roman Castle (1180 CE): attempted to bring ties between the Armenian and Roman Catholic churches
- Tarsus (1196 CE): attempted to bring ties between the Armenian and Roman Catholic churches
- Sis I (1307 CE): attempted to unite the Armenian church with the Roman Catholic church
- Sis II (1343 CE): attempted to untie the Armenian church with the Roman Catholic church

bishops who insisted on the patriarchal residence remaining in Cilicia, which resulted a schism.

The Armenian Church in the Medieval Era

During the patriarchy of Catholicos Constantine I (1221-1267 CE), there was a strong attempt at uniting the Armenian Church with Rome. This occurred during the reign of Kings Leo II and Hethum I, who were great supporters of Rome. This began the process of latinizing the Armenian Church. Those who remained faithful to their Eastern dogma elected another patriarch. As a result, there were two patriarchs for the Armenian Church and this continued to be the case until the fall of Cilicia at the hands of the Egyptian Mamluks in 1375 CE.

This caused a division in the Armenian Church, with one group (not supporting Roman influence), which restored the historical patriarchal residence in Etchmiadzin in the mountains of Armenia and another group supporting Rome with its patriarchal residence in Sis, which was established in 1293 CE. This meant that two Catholicoi headed the church and each began to shepherd specific regions where Armenians dwelt. In 1311 CE, the Armenian bishop of Jerusalem was granted the title patriarch. Following him was the bishop of the eparchy of Constantinople who was granted the title "patriarch" after Constantinople became a patriarchate in 1461 CE.[139]

---

[139] Despite this patriarchate being originally under the Catholicos of Sis, the administrative and state power of the patriarch residing in Istanbul

Due to the flourishing status of Istanbul, Armenians began immigrating to Istanbul where they assumed important occupations within the Ottoman Empire. They established churches and hospitals and were active members in the flourishing and development of the Ottoman capital from a financial and an architectural perspective.

On another front, the inclination toward establishing ties between the Roman Catholic Church and the Armenian Church did not stop. Armenians sent delegates to the Council of Florence. The Catholicization of the Armenian Church was on the rise throughout the seventeenth and eighteenth centuries. The Armenian bishop of Aleppo, Abraham Arzivian, was Catholic in faith. In 1740 CE, he was appointed Catholicos over Sis, which caused a schism within the Armenian Church in his eparchy with one Orthodox sect and another Catholic sect. The young patriarch then organized his millet despite Turkish disagreement. His diocese included Cilicia, Syria, and Egypt. The rest of the Armenian Catholics in Turkey were under the papal vicar in Constantinople until Pope Pius VIII appointed an Armenian Archbishop directly associated with the Apostolic See in Rome.

The most important event in the sixteenth century in the Armenian Church was the establishment of a printing house in Etchmiadzin with the efforts of Catholicos Michael I (1564-1571 CE) who sent Abkar the monk to Italy to learn

---

was much stronger as the Ottoman government granted him the task of shepherding the Armenian, Syrian and Chaldean Christians in Istanbul.

the art of printing. This monk was able to establish Armenian printing houses in Venice, Rome, Constantinople, Etchmiadzin, Isfahan, and Amsterdam. The Armenian Bible was printed in its entirety with the efforts of Bishop Oskan.

The Armenian Church in the Modern Era

With the dawn of the eighteenth century, the Persian Empire began to deteriorate. By the middle of the eighteenth century (1748 CE), Armenia was divided between the Persians and Ottomans which scattered the Armenian people in Cilicia, North Syria, Iraq, and Asia Minor. The center site for Armenians remained in Constantinople though the role of the Patriarch was limited. In such a manner, Armenian history began to deteriorate and fall. The presence of schisms and divisions opened the door for Western missionaries in the eighteenth century, taking advantage of French protection through the French ambassador in Constantinople. Under the influence of the French ambassador, the Armenian Patriarch Avedik I was arrested, trialed by inquisitors, and sentenced to death in France in 1711 CE.

In 1867 CE, Sis and Istanbul were merged into one eparchy under the Patriarchate in Istanbul. After the French retreated from Cecilia, the Catholicos of Sis had to leave Turkey with whoever was left in the congregation and became refugees in Lebanon, where he established his residence in Antelias in Lebanon near the capital.

As such, the Armenian Church was administratively found in two bodies: a Church with its residence in

Etchmiadzin in Armenia, and the see of Cilicia with its residence in Antelias with both patriarchs carrying the title of Catholicos.

In 1956 CE, the Cilician Church in Lebanon divided itself from the See of Etchmiadzin accusing the latter of succumbing to communist rule. Since 1983 CE, the relations between the two centers improved yet the Church in Lebanon refused the suggestions presented by the Church in Etchmiadzin in 1980 CE. These suggestions entailed that the Church of Sis or Cilicia give up the title of Catholicos to indicate its equality with the See of Etchmiadzin and become a Patriarch equal to the Patriarchs in Jerusalem and Constantinople.[140]

The Armenian Church has witnessed a social and spiritual revival that began with the beginning of the second half of the 20th century that continues to this day. More than 40 bishops were ordained until 1984 CE inside and outside Armenia. Many ancient Churches and monasteries were renewed. Many books and religious encyclicals were produced and the Church began having its own publishing press which publishes the monthly encyclical titled "Etchmiadzin," the annual Church calendar, Armenian religious books, and the New Testament in Armenia. In

---

[140] When the Ottomans took over in 1517, they acknowledged the Armenian Patriarch of Constantinople as a civil leader of all Armenians while also acknowledging the Patriarchate of Jerusalem. Despite that, the Armenian Church was subject to severe persecution and genocide. The Armenian Church experienced great atrocities and tragedies under the Turkish yoke.

addition, there is a theological revival led by the theological seminary in Etchmiadzin.

In September 1983 CE, after the preparation of the holy chrism, the Patriarch with Church hierarchs and a large number of Armenians headed to the tomb of the Armenian martyrs. The Catholicos placed a crown of flowers next to the lamp that always burns beside their tomb. A memorial service was held for the repose of the souls of 1.5 million Armenian martyrs who lost their lives sixty years earlier in Western Armenia and Turkey.

In 1990 CE, the Armenian Church celebrated its 350th anniversary of the theological seminary in Etchmiadzin in Armenia. This theological school was inaugurated between 1637 and 1649 CE during the Patriarchate of Catholicos Philip (1633 – 1655 CE).

Since Armenia has regained its independence from the Soviet Union in September 1991 CE, the Armenian Church has enjoyed absolute freedom. In 1995 CE, after the repose of Catholicos Vazgen I, Catholicos Karekin I was chosen to succeed him. His Holiness was enthroned in April of the same year as the 131st Catholicos of Etchmiadzin. In July of the same year, Aram I Keshishian, the Metropolitan of Lebanon for the Armenian Orthodox, was chosen as Catholicos of Cilicia. He was enthroned in the Cathedral of Antelias with the rite of the Armenian Church. For the first time, the Catholicos of Etchmiadzin attended the enthronement together with the patriarchs of Jerusalem and Constantinople. The enthronement was also attended by HH

Pope Shenouda III, the Alexandrian Pope, and Abune Paulos, the Ethiopian Patriarch.

Currently, there are Armenian Orthodox metropolis in Cairo, Baghdad, Isfahan, Tabriz, Tehran, Kolkata, Bucharest, Paris, Marseille, New York, Los Angeles, Buenos Aires, in addition to the Catholicate of Sis, and the Patriarchates of Jerusalem and Constantinople. These metropolises serve Armenian immigrants spread across the diaspora.

Bibliography and Further Readings

Agadjanian, Alexander, ed. Armenian Christianity Today: Identity Politics and Popular Practice. Farnham: Ashgate, 2014.

Allen, Pauline, and C. T. R. Hayward. *Severus of Antioch*. 1 edition. London: Routledge, 2005.

Arpee, Leon. *A History of Armenian Christianity from the Beginning to Our Own Time*. New York: The Armenian Missionary Association of America, Inc., 1946.

Asale, Bruk A. "The Ethiopian Orthodox Tewahedo Church Canon of the Scriptures: Neither Open nor Closed." *The Bible Translator* 67, no. 2 (August 1, 2016): 202–22. https://doi.org/10.1177/2051677016651486.

Athanasius Al-Makari. Al-Kanais Al-Sharkeya wa Awtanaha "The Eastern Churches and Their Homelands." Dar Nobar; Cairo: Egypt, 2000.

Atiya, Aziz Suryal. *A History of Eastern Christianity*. London: Methuen, 1968.

Ayele Teklehaymanot. *The Ethiopian Church and Its Christological Doctrine*. Rev. English ed. Addis Ababa: Graphic Printers, 1982.

Aymro Wondmagegnehu, and Joachim Motovu. *The Ethiopian Orthodox Church*. Addis Abada: Ethiopian Orthodox Mission, 1970.

Bcheiry, Iskandar. The Account of the Syriac Orthodox Patriarch Yūḥanun Bar Šay Allah (1483-1492): The Syriac Manuscript of Cambridge: DD.3.8(1). Gorgias Eastern Christian Studies 34. Piscataway: Gorgias Press, 2013.

Behr, John. *The Nicene Faith*. Formation of Christian Theology, v. 2. Crestwood: St. Vladimir's Seminary Press, 2004.

Bell, David N. *Orthodoxy: Evolving Tradition*. Cistercian Studies Series, no. 228. Trappist: Cistercian Publications, 2008.

Beshara, Amgad. *Qisat Al-Hob Al-'ajib "The Story of Wondrous Love."* First. Cairo: Dar-Salam, 2017.

Binns, John. The Orthodox Church of Ethiopia: A History. London: Bloomsbury Publishing, 2016.

Bishop Poemen of Malawi. *Articles on Orthodox Spirituality*. Malawi: Al-Kanisah Al-Morqoseyah, 1972.

Bishop Poemen of Malawi. *The Orthodox Vision of the World*. Cairo: al-Mahaba Publishing Press.

Brooks, E. W. The Sixth Book of the Select Letters of Severus, Patriarch of Antioch; In the Syriac Version of Athanasius of Nisibis; Vol. II. (Translation) Part II, Pp. 231-480. Leopold Classic Library, 2016.

Conlin, Patrick. "Eradicating the Root of Hatred: The Development of Bar Hebraeus; Ecumenism." *UWM Religious Studies Student Organization 2019 Conference: Religion and the Human Condition*. Accessed December 7, 2019. https://www.academia.edu/37843603/Eradicating_the_Root_of_Hatred_The_Development_of_Bar_Hebraeuss_Ecumenism.

Cyril of Alexandria, Nicholas P. Lunn, and Gregory K. Hillis. *Glaphyra on the Pentateuch*. Fathers of the Church: A New Translation, volume 137, 138. Washington, D.C: The Catholic University of America Press, 2018.

Cyril of Alexandria, David R. Maxwell, trans., and Joel C. Elowsky, ed. *Commentary on John*. Ancient Christian Texts. Downers Grove: InterVarsity Press, 2015.

Cyril of Alexandria, and John Anthony McGuckin. *On the Unity of Christ*. Popular Patristics Series, no. 13. Crestwood: St. Vladimir's Seminary Press, 1995.

Cyril of Alexandria. *'Hiwar 'Hawl Al-Thalouth "Dialogues on the Trinity."* Translated by Joseph Faltas. Cairo: The Institute of St. Anthony, 2014.

Daoud, Marcus, trans. *The Liturgy of the Ethiopian Church*. New York : Philadelphia: Routledge Taylor & Francis Group [Distributor], 2005. http://myaccess.library.utoronto.ca/login?url=https://www.taylorfrancis.com/books/9780203040904.

Day, Peter D. Eastern Christian Liturgies: The Armenian, Coptic, Ethiopian, and Syrian Rites; Eucharistic Rites with Introductory Notes and Rubrical Instructions. Shannon: Irish University Press, 1972.

Dinno, Khalid S. "The Syrian Orthodox Christians in the Late Ottoman and Post-Ottoman Periods: Crisis and Revival." *Dissertation Abstracts International*. Accessed July 28, 2018. http://resource.library.utoronto.ca/eir/EIRdetail.cfm?Resources_ID=1857524.

Domnic, Negussie Andre. *The Fetha Nagast and Its Ecclesiology: Implications in Ethiopian Catholic Church Today*. Europäische Hochschulschriften. Reihe XXIII, Theologie = Publications Universitaires Europeennes. Série 23, Theologie = European University Studies. Series 23, Theology, Bd. 910. Bern ; New York: Peter Lang, 2010.

"Eritrean Christians Suffering Persecution." *Canadian Mennonite; Waterloo*, June 14, 2004.

Ervine, Roberta R., and St. Nersess Armenian Seminary, eds. Worship Traditions in Armenia and the Neighboring Christian East: An International Symposium in Honor of the 40th Anniversary of St. Nersess Armenian Seminary. Avant Series, bk. 3. Crestwood, N.Y.: St. Vladimir's Seminary Press ; St. Nersess Armenian Seminary, 2006.

"Ethiopian Biblical Interpretation: A Study in Exegetical Tradition and Hermeneutics / | University of Toronto Libraries." Accessed July 28, 2018. https://search.library.utoronto.ca/details?1795132&uuid=7b0b7082-0ae4-44aa-a1ee-85e6c843b57f.

Ethiopian Church: Treasures & Faith. Forcalquier] : [Addis Ababa: Ethiopian Orthodox Tewahido Church, 2009.

Fritsch, Emmanuel. The Liturgical Year of the Ethiopian Church: The Temporal: Seasons and Sundays. Ethiopian review of cultures v. 9-10. [Ethiopia: s.n.], 2001.

Gebru, Mebratu Kiros. *Miaphysite Christology*. Piscataway: Gorgias Press, 2010.

Gebru, Mebratu Kiros. Miaphysite Christology: A Study of the Ethiopian Tewahedo Christological Tradition on the Nature of Christ. Canadian Thesis, MR-09886. Ottawa: Library and Archives Canada, 2006.

"Glory and Burden : Ministry and Sacraments of the Church / | University of Toronto Libraries." Accessed December 7, 2019.

https://search.library.utoronto.ca/details?9255410&uuid=e7a370d8-8d47-45b6-abdb-85d7f22e549a.

Habtemariam, Semere. Reflections on the History of the Abyssinian Orthodox Tewahdo Church. Trenton: Africa World Press, 2017.

Hepner, Tricia Redeker. "Religion, Nationalism, and Transnational Civil Society in the Eritrean Diaspora." *Identities* 10, no. 3 (2003): 269–93. https://doi.org/10.1080/10702890390228874.

Hovorun, Cyril. Will, Action, and Freedom: Christological Controversies in the Seventh Century. Medieval Mediterranean, v. 77. Leiden: Brill, 2008.

Hyatt, Harry Middleton. *The Church of Abyssinia*. Oriental Research Series, v. 4. London: Luzac, 1928.

Ighnāṭyūs Afrām. *History of the Syriac Dioceses*. 1st ed. Publications of the Archdiocese of the Syriac Orthodox Church in the Eastern United States 3. Piscataway: Gorgias Press, Beth Antioch Press, 2009.

Ighnāṭyūs Afrām. *The Shorter Catechism of the Syrian Orthodox Church of Antioch*. Teaneck: Reprinted by The Archdiocese of the Syrian Orthodox Church for the Eastern USA, 1999.

Isaac, Ephraim. *The Ethiopian Orthodox Täwahïdo Church*. Afroasiatic Studies, no. 1. Trenton: Red Sea Press, 2012.

Isaac, Ephraim, and Marjorie LeMay. *The Ethiopian Church*. Boston: H. N. Sawyer Co, 1967.

Kaniamparampil, Curian Corepiscopa. *The Syrian Orthodox Church in India and Its Apostolic Faith*. Tiruvalla, Kerala, India: National Offset Press / Rev. Philips Gnanasikhamony, 1989. http://archive.org/details/syrianorthodoxch0000kani

Karekin. *In Search of Spiritual Life: An Armenian Christian Miscellany*. Antelias: Armenian Catholicosate of Cilicia, 1991.

K'ēshishean, Aram. Saint Nerses the Gracious and Church Unity: Armeno-Greek Church Relations, 1165-1173. Antilias: Armenian Catholicosate of Cilicia, 2010.

K'ēshishean, Aram. *The Armenian Church: An Introduction to Armenian Christianity*. Second edition. Antelias: Armenian Catholicosate of Cilicia, 2017.

Krikorian, Mesrob K. Christology of the Oriental Orthodox Churches: Christology in the Tradition of the Armenian Apostolic Church.

Frankfurt am Main: Peter Lang GmbH, Internationaler Verlag der Wissenschaften, 2010.

Malaty, Fr Tadros Y. "THE SCHOOL OF ALEXANDRIA-Book One; BEFORE ORIGEN," n.d.

Malaty, Tadrous Y. *Introduction to the Coptic Orthodox Church*. Sporting: St. George's Coptic Orthodox Church, 1993.

Marsh, Richard, ed. Prayers from the East: Traditions of Eastern Christianity. Minneapolis: Fortress Press, 2004.

Matthew, Austin F., ed. *The Teaching of the Abyssinian Church*. London: Faith Press, 1936.

McGuckin, John Anthony, and Cyril. St. Cyril of Alexandria: The Christological Controversy; Its History, Theology, and Texts. Crestwood: St. Vladimir's Seminary Press, 2004.

Meinardus, Otto F. A. *Christian Egypt, Faith and Life*. Cairo: American University in Cairo Press, 1970.

Meinardus, Otto F. A. *Two Thousand Years of Coptic Christianity*. Second paperback edition. Cairo: The American University in Cairo Press, 2015.

Meyendorff, John. *Imperial Unity and Christian Divisions: The Church, 450-680 A.D.* Church in History 2. Crestwood: St. Vladimir's Seminary Press, 1989.

Moss, Yonatan. *Incorruptible Bodies: Christology, Society, and Authority in Late Antiquity*. First edition. Oakland: University of California Press, 2016.

Oden, Thomas C. The African Memory of Mark: Reassessing Early Church Tradition. Downers Grove: IVP Academic, 2011.

Orthodox Unity (Orthodox Joint Commission). "Orthodox Unity (Orthodox Joint Commission)." Accessed November 8, 2019. https://orthodoxjointcommission.wordpress.com/.

O'Hanlon, Douglas. *Features of the Abyssinian Church*. London: Society for Promoting Christian Knowledge, 1946.

O'Leary, De Lacy. *The Ethiopian Church: Historical Notes on the Church of Abyssinia*. London: Society for Promoting Christian Knowledge, 1936.

Papazian, Iris. *Karekin I In His Own Words*. Vagharashapat: Kerakin I Theological and Armenological Studies Series, 2002.

Paulos Gregorios. *A Human God*. First. Kerala: Mar Gregorios Foundation, 1992.

Paulos Gregorios. Glory and Burden: Ministry and Sacraments of the Church. Delhi: ISPCK/MGF, 2005.

Paulos Gregorios, and Gregory. Cosmic Man: The Divine Presence: The Theology of St. Gregory of Nyssa (ca. 330 to ca. 395 A.D.). New York: Paragon House, 1988.

Paulos Gregorios. *Paulos Mar Gregorios: A Reader*. Edited by K. M. George. Minneapolis: Fortress Press, 2017.

Pelikan, Jaroslav Jan, and Jaroslav Jan Pelikan. *The Emergence of the Catholic Tradition (100-600)*. Christian Tradition 1. Chicago: University of Chicago Press, 1971.

Phillipson, D. W. *Ancient Churches of Ethiopia: Four-Fourteenth Centuries*. New Haven: Yale University Press, 2009.

Poor, Fr Matthew the. *Guidelines for Prayers*. Wadi Al-Natroun: St. Macarius Monastery, 2016.

Pope Shenouda III. *Ro'haneyet Al-Soum "Spirituality of Fasting."* Cairo: St. Ruiss Al-Abaseya, 1983.

Pseudo-Dionysius the Areopagite, *Pseudo-Dionysius: The Complete Works.* Trans. Colum Luibheid. Mawah: Paulist Press, 1987.

Saint-Laurent, Jeanne-Nicole Mellon. *Missionary Stories and the Formation of the Syriac Churches*. Transformation of the Classical Heritage 55. Oakland: University of California Press, 2015.

Schaff, Philip. *Nicene and Post-Nicene Fathers*. 1 edition. Peabody: Hendrickson Publishers, 1990.

Sergew Hable Selassie, and Ya'Ityopyā 'ortodoks tawāḥedo béta kerestiyān, eds. *The Church of Ethiopia: A Panorama of History and Spiritual Life*. Addis Ababa: Ethiopian Orthodox Church, 1970.

Severus of Antioch, Athanasius, and Ernest Walter Brooks. The Sixth Book of the Select Letters of Severus, Patriarch of Antioch, in the Syriac Version of Athanasius of Nisibis, Edited and Translated by E. W. Brooks: Pt. 1-2. Text. Ulan Press, 2012.

Severus of Antioch. *Al-Khateyah Al-Jedyah "Ancestral Sin."* Translated by George Farag. Saint Athanasius Fellowship, 2019

Syriac Orthodox Church, and Syriac Orthodox Church, eds. *Slawāthā D-Ramshā Wa-d-Safrā =: Evening and Morning Prayers: According to the Rite of the Syriac Orthodox Church of Antioch.* [Teaneck, N.J: Archdiocese of the Syriac Orthodox Church for the Eastern USA], 2002.

Syrian Orthodox Church, Athanasius Yeshue Samuel, and Murad Saliba Barsom, eds. *Ma'de'dono: the book of the church festivals according to the ancient rite of the Syrian Orthodox Church of Antioch.* Lodi: Mar Athanasius Yeshue Samuel, 1984.

Terian, Abraham. The Festal Works of St. Gregory of Narek: Annotated Translation of the Odes, Litanies, and Encomia. Collegeville: Pueblo Books, 2016.

"The Christian Church and Missions in Ethiopia : Including Eritrea and the Somali lands/ | University of Toronto Libraries." Accessed July 28, 2018. https://search.library.utoronto.ca/details?181706&uuid=3005122e-0a10-47de-bf04-ec442eadd2a5.

"The Ethiopian Orthodox Church : A Contribution to the Ecumenical Study of Less Known Eastern Churches / | University of Toronto Libraries." Accessed July 28, 2018. https://search.library.utoronto.ca/details?8829871&uuid=7b0b7082-0ae4-44aa-a1ee-85e6c843b57f.

Thomson, Robert W. *Studies in Armenian Literature and Christianity*. Collected Studies CS451. Altershot: Variorum, 1994.

Tootikian, Vahan H. *Highlights of Armenian Christendom*. Southfield: Armenian Evangelical World Council and Armenian Heritage Committee, 2002.

Torrance, Iain R. Christology after Chalcedon: Severus of Antioch and Sergius the Monophysite. Norwich: Canterbury Press, 1988.

Touma Issa, Boutros, ed. *Readings in the 20th Century Genocide of the Syriac Orthodox Church of Antioch (Sayfo)*. Religion and Society. New York: Nova Science Publishers, Inc, 2017.

"Traditional Ethiopian Church Education / | University of Toronto Libraries." Accessed July 28, 2018. https://search.library.utoronto.ca/details?2568266&uuid=7b0b7082-0ae4-44aa-a1ee-85e6c843b57f.

Watson, John H. *Among the Copts*. Brighton: Sussex Academic Press, 2000.

"Worship in the Syriac Orthodox Church." http://sor.cua.edu/Worship/index.html.

Yesehaq. The Structure and Practice of the Ethiopian Church Liturgy. Bronx, N.Y: E.O.C, 1983.

"دائرة الدراسات السريانية – لا فَخرَ للكنيسةِ إلّا بِكثرةِ الكُتبِ." https://dss-syriacpatriarchate.org/.

About the Author

Andrew N.A. Youssef was awarded his MTS by the Orthodox School of Theology at Trinity College and continued his studies as a PhD Candidate at Toronto School of Theology. Andrew is a chaplain in a hospital in the City of Toronto and is a member of the Canadian Association for Spiritual Care.

www.ingramcontent.com/pod-product-compliance
Lightning Source LLC
Chambersburg PA
CBHW030515080526
44586CB00011B/198